# Trinidad: Looking Back From My Front Porch

John Meyers

Copyright © 2016 by John Meyers

All rights reserved

ISBN 13: 978-1533194602

ISBN 10: 1533194602

All rights reserved. No part of this book may be reproduced or transmitted in any form or by any means, electronic or mechanical, including photocopying, recording, or by any information storage and retrieval system, without permission in writing from the copyright owner.

Photos used by permission:

Trinidad Museum Society

A.W. Erickson Collection Humboldt State University Library

Cover photo, Plank Houses and Granite Cross by John Meyers

To order additional copies of this book, contact:

Moss Canyon
www.mosscanyon.com

# Table of Contents

Introduction ................................................................................. vi
Me' womenee - Principios – Beginnings ............................... 9
Trapping and Trading and Gold… Oh, My! ......................... 16
You Have Mail ......................................................................... 26
Gold Bluff… bluff… ................................................................ 27
Hey, Look at Them Big Trees ................................................. 31
Indian Trouble… or was it White Man trouble? ................... 36
What Gold? ............................................................................... 38
Sawmills to the Rescue ........................................................... 39
Patrick's Point ......................................................................... 44
Can I Have an Amen to That? ................................................ 45
Now that's Entertainment! ..................................................... 47
Grave Matters .......................................................................... 48
Schools ..................................................................................... 49
Fish ........................................................................................... 49
Ship Building .......................................................................... 50
Indian Wars ............................................................................. 51
The Bald Hills ......................................................................... 55
Bull o' the Woods ................................................................... 56
Officially a Town… a City… no wait, a Town… ................ 61
Trinidad Becomes a City with a Lighthouse ........................ 62
Do You Smell Smoke? ............................................................ 64
Railroads and Roads and Cars… Oh My! ............................ 67
Where'd the Town Go? ........................................................... 77
Doc, My Arm Hurts in Three Places ..................................... 79
Watch the Cow ........................................................................ 80

The Big Storm ........................................................................ 80
Do You Smell Smoke? ......................................................... 80
The Last Ship ....................................................................... 83
More Mills ............................................................................. 83
The Lighthouse and the Wave ............................................. 86
Keep on Movin' On ............................................................. 88
The Last Yurok in Tsurai ..................................................... 91
One Last Tsurai Story ......................................................... 92
Westhaven is Born .............................................................. 93
Trinidad Keeps Going .......................................................... 93
Thar She Blows! ................................................................... 94
Killed By an Apple ............................................................... 99
Asphalt Comes to Trinidad ................................................. 99
Rock on! ............................................................................. 100
Oh, the Power! ................................................................... 102
Standard Oil ....................................................................... 104
The Legend of Judas and the Sheep ............................... 104
Passing of an Era ............................................................... 105
Do You Smell Smoke? ....................................................... 106
The War Years ................................................................... 106
The Pier .............................................................................. 108
Earthquakes! ...................................................................... 109
The End? ............................................................................ 110
Trinidad Sawmills .............................................................. 112
Map ..................................................................................... 113
Nautical Terms ................................................................... 114

# Introduction

I'm not a Trinidad native. I'm not even a Humboldt County native, but after living in Trinidad for thirty years, I've heard lots of colorful stories about its history and so I decided that it was time for me to check some of them out. That turned out to be a little harder than I thought. Don't get me wrong, there are lots of facts out there... they just don't all match up.

When I started this book, I quickly discovered that for every story I'd been told, there were three or four versions of it in a variety of articles and books and online (and we all know that they can't put it online unless it's true...), and no two sources were the same in details. Plus, I wanted to tell the story my way, not just copy what someone else had already written.

Therefore, this book, which is intended to be a brief history of the area, is my best attempt to sort out the stories based on what I've been told and what I read in books, articles and letters. I do not vouch for the absolute accuracy of dates. I did my best.

Many thanks to Patti Fleschner and the Trinidad Museum for plenty of assistance.

The Humboldt Room at the Humboldt County Library main branch also has many reference books on the subject, so thank you to them as well. The Humboldt County Clerk's office was very helpful with records, too. And let's not forget the Humboldt County Historical Society!

And, of course, my wife, Sheryl, who helped with research and editing all my mistakes of which were grammatical in form, and speling...seriously?

My intention was to write this book as though you and I were sitting on the front porch and, in my old age, I'm just telling interesting and fun stories that I remember. I also tried to keep the whole thing in a somewhat chronological timeline… but I'm easily distracted by shiny objects and Oh! Squirrel!

The nautical terms section is included because after living here for about twenty years, it occurred to me that I didn't really know anything about nautical terms. I decided to fix that. And now I'm sharing my newfound wealth of knowledge with you!

## Me' womenee - Principios – Beginnings
(Yurok – Spanish – English)

The thriving city of Trinidad, California, elevation one hundred and seventy-four feet, is located on the southern end of the prehistoric ancestral land of the Oohl people. The Oohl were given the name 'Yurok' from the Karuk language[1] – Yurok literally means 'downriver'... the river referred to being the Klamath, and so that's the name that we use. However, the Oohl people simply referred to themselves as Olekwo'l, which means 'persons'. If they were from down river on the Klamath they were Pue-lik-lo', which means 'Down River People', and people on the upper Klamath and Trinity were Pey-cheek-lo', which means 'Up River People' - and people on the coast were Ner-'er-ner' - Coast People.

The Oohl came to this area around 1100 A.D. having been proceeded by the Wiyots who showed up around 900 A.D. and the Karuk sometime even before that. The Tolowa, Hupa, Chilula, and Whilkut people all arrived around 1300 A.D., so they all have some history here. The Oohl had more than fifty villages with a population of something around three thousand people spread over their ancestral land, which covered the area from the Klamath and Trinity Rivers to the coast down to Little River at Clam Beach. The Wiyots set up house south of that,

---
[1] The Karuk's were neighbors of the Oohl.

with the Chilula and Hupa to the east of the Wiyots, the Karuk to the east of the Oohl, and the Tolowa on the north end of them all.

The Oohl language was spoken along Klamath River, but along the coast south of the mouth of the river there were three different dialects; one spoken at Gold Bluff, one at Redwood Creek, and a third at Tsurai, which was the most different from the main language... maybe it was their version of the southern drawl. The Wiyots and Karuks and others all had different languages. For us, it would be like each California County having its own language.

The Ner-'er-ner' established the village of Tsurai, which is pronounced *'chure-eye'*, and which means 'mountain' in the Yurok language, on the southernmost end of Yurok territory sometime between the 1100's and 1600's – sources vary, but I personally believe it was much earlier than the 1600's figure. An anthropologist named Kroebler came up with that date. Several sources place it in a 'prehistoric' category. In any case, it was established well before it was found by Spanish explorers in the 1700's. The village was on the brushy bluffs above the beach water line with the high Head[2] next to it that provided a protected fishing area. By the time the Spanish arrived, the village itself consisted of ten or twelve redwood Plank Houses, a sweat house, a dance hall,[3] a boat landing, and a graveyard. The Ner-'er-ner' managed to live a quiet life of fishing, canoe making and basket weaving for a long time before we showed up.

The Yuroks didn't have a 'chief'. Each village had more of a control family that included a rich man who was very important because his wealth consisted mostly of dance costumes, such as white deerskins and woodpecker scalps, and shell money,[4] so there couldn't be any religious ceremonies without him because he possessed all the costumes; but he wasn't regarded as the

---

[2] You can look it up in the Nautical Terms section at the back of this book.
[3] No piano player... it was for ceremonial dances.
[4] Their money was 'Dentalia', a type of sea shell.

head-man possessing authority. The last rich man of Tsurai was a man named Morwene, otherwise known as Mau.[5]

Housing consisted of redwood Plank Houses,[6] which were built by many North Coast tribes up to and through most of the 19th century. Typically the houses were about twenty feet by twenty feet square and six or seven feet high. The planks were split from naturally fallen trees or removed from large standing trees, allowing the tree to heal and remain alive. Inside the walls, they dug out the whole area about four feet deep, and this is where the family lived - cooking, sleeping and doing family stuff. In Yurok culture, the men didn't sleep in these family houses. Instead, they spent their nights in sweat houses.

Plank Houses at Sumeg Village
Tsurai was one of the largest Yurok villages

---

[5] Mau died in the late 1800's. He was over one hundred years old.
[6] You can see the plank houses pictured at Sumeg village in Patrick's Point State Park.

There's a historic marker[7] overlooking the bluff in Trinidad where the village was located that states:

*"Directly below was located the ancient Yurok village of Tsurai. A prehistoric, permanent Indian community, it was first discovered by Captains Bodega and Heceta, June 9-19, 1775. The houses were of hand-split redwood planks, designed for defense and protection. The village was occupied until 1916."*

It's above what we now call 'Indian Beach'. The descendants of the villagers call it 'Old Home Beach'. The word 'Indian' wasn't used by the Yuroks either, of course. We got that word from Columbus, who was searching for the 'Indias' which was how the Europeans referred to all of South and East Asia. When he landed in the Caribbean, he thought he was in Asia, so he called the natives he found there, "Indians", and the name stuck.

But that's off my story.

The first known sighting of this harbor by Europeans was in the 1500's when the galleon *Manila* sailed past under the command of Spanish explorer, Captain Sebastian Rodriguez Cermeño. Cermeño didn't land here, but he reported the harbor and Head, which led to the Ner-'er-ner' peoples' discovery of Europeans as more ships followed and did land.

Despite what the sign says, the Spanish didn't 'discover' the village of Tsurai. It wasn't lost... the Yuroks knew exactly where it was all along.

By the mid-1700's, the Russians were showing a lot of interest in the northern parts of the coast, which was worrying the Spanish who had made claim and established holdings along the southern parts, so in order to cut the Russians off at the pass, as it were, the Spanish Court sent captains Bruno de Heceta (Hezeta) y Dudagoitia of the ship *Santiago*, and Juan Francisco de la Bodega y Quadra of the ship *Sonora* on a special

---

[7] From the corner of Trinity and Edwards Street, face the bay and then look to your left. The marker is up at the turn of the street.

mission. They anchored their ships in the harbor on June 9, 1775 with instructions to claim the land for Spain – which they did, two days after landing. On Trinity Sunday, a formal act of possession was conducted by the Spanish sailors. They dressed up in fancy uniforms with lots of ribbons and medals and had a big ceremony with flowery speeches and they fired off their noisy cannons and erected a large wooden cross on the Head[8] that had the inscription:

*"Carolus III Dei G. Hyspaniarum Rex"*

… which translates to; "in the name of King Carlos of Spain." They proclaimed the area as 'La Santisima Trinidad' (the Holy Trinity), and that's how the European name for the village of Tsurai and its bay became 'Trinidad'. I'm sure the villagers were duly impressed as they stood there shaking their heads and saying, "Well, I guess this is their land now. I told you we should have put up a no trespassing sign!"

The members of the expedition described the Indians they met as 'affable' and most likely, the villagers initially saw the Spanish sailors as potential trading partners… except for one little incident.

There's a story that the first actual European settler in our area was one of the sailors from either Heceta or Bodega y Quadra's ship who 'fell in love' with a native girl and jumped ship to stay with her. The Spanish captains didn't take kindly to this and Heceta, much to the disapproval of his fellow officers, conducted a search for the missing sailor through the village in a hot-headed shake-down, but the villagers didn't take it to heart. They still liked the Spanish visitors.

A young boy about five or ten years old, named Morwene witnessed the Spaniard's landing…remember that name? He ended up as the last rich man of Tsurai. How impressive the

---

[8] There's a concrete memorial cross there now. Hike up the trail/road on the east side of the Head. Remains of the original wooden cross are on display in the Trinidad Museum.

Spaniard's ships must have been to the young Mau, with their billowing white sails and immense size compared to the Yurok's canoes; and then the strange men in their odd clothes and speech that made no sense. They didn't speak Karuk or Wiyot or any language Mau had ever heard. Yet the villagers were able to communicate and trade with them, having no idea of what was to come in the long run from welcoming these strange men to their village.

This was 1775. Consider that just a year later, in 1776, a group of rebellious colonists fed up with rule by England, signed a Declaration of Independence on the other side of the country and started up a war with England, which we won, and George Washington became our president.

Yeah... meanwhile, back in Trinidad...

The Spanish claimed the land, but they didn't really do any follow-up and establish a physical presence here. If they had, I'd be writing this in Spanish, which would look like gibberish because I don't speak Spanish. By the early 1800's, Trinidad Bay, since it was pretty much the *only* stop along the north coast, was a regular stop for English and Spanish sea-going fur traders who were conducting Chinese trade expeditions. The Chinese were extremely interested in the fur trade with the European ships that landed here to resupply and to gather what seal and sea otter and other furs they could. Ships and their crews also prowled the coast looking for other sheltered harbors like Trinidad Bay to use for access to the inland fur trading routes, but they weren't having much luck.

In fact, early explorers including Sir Francis Drake, Juan Francisco de la Bodega y Quadra and George Vancouver sailed right past Humboldt Bay, to our south, while mapping the coast and looking for a mythical cross-continental passage. Vancouver anchored in Trinidad Bay in 1793, but wasn't impressed. He did note the Spanish cross and claim on the land, though.

In 1804, William Shaler and the American ship *Leila Byrd* sailed from Canton, China - where seal skins sold anywhere from eighty cents to two dollars while an otter fur brought from thirty dollars to as much as a hundred and twenty dollars - to the mouth of the Columbia River to resupply, but he couldn't make the bar crossing, so he sailed on south, anchoring in Trinidad Bay. It was the first American ship to land here.

In 1805, Captain Jonathon Winship and the ship *O'Cain* located what he named 'Washington Inlet'… what we now call Big Lagoon, and the Yurok called 'O Ket'uel'… and then anchored in Trinidad Bay. A year later, 1806, he returned in the *O'Cain* and finally located … discovered…luckily stumbled upon… the entrance to the bay south of Trinidad and made the first recorded entry into what would eventually become 'Humboldt Bay'. Winship was all excited about his discovery and proceeded to name the bay the 'Bay of Rezanov' since he was partnered with the Russian-American Company[9] at the time. But, incredibly, he failed to map the bay entrance when he left! Oops.

All the ships looking for another port south of Trinidad had been missing that bay inlet partially because the opening is fairly small; it's actually referred to as the 'jaws', where a five foot swell[10] can compress against the outgoing tide and double or triple in size in a very short time, which can lead to breakers[11] at three to four second intervals that can be ten to twelve feet high. The Humboldt Bay bar crossing is considered the second most dangerous on the west coast, with the Columbia River being the worst; and then you have to travel up a channel to actually reach the open bay. Add that to the fact that the inlet was usually covered by rain and dense, soupy, impenetrable fog – what we like to call zero-zero visibility - and you can see why it was hard to find. So when Winship failed to map it, the entrance was lost once again. Mother nature was still protecting her own.

---

[9] The Russian-American Company was a Russian Company charged with colonizing Russian America in 1799.
[10] Again, in the back of this book.
[11] You got it… in the back of the book.

Compare that to Trinidad Bay that has the three hundred and eighty foot high Head to the west, and Pilot Rock[12] which is more than three hundred feet across the base and over ninety feet above the water, to the south. The whole length of the breakwater there is about two thousand six hundred feet with an average depth from shore to rock of about seven to eight fathoms.[13] What all this means is; there's no dangerous bar crossing like in Humboldt Bay… and it's plenty deep without any dredging.

For the Yuroks, trading with the Europeans for supplies and furs continued uneasily and sometimes under the threat of gunfire with boat cannons pointed directly at the village. And it only got worse into the 1800's as the new Americans arrived in the area. Trinidad Bay was perfectly located pretty much halfway between San Francisco Bay and the mouth of the Columbia River, which was an important fur trading area since Lewis and Clark made it famous in 1805. American Robert Grey was actually the first to go up the river in 1792. However, by 1808, the sea otters around here had already almost been depleted by the trade.

## Trapping and Trading and Gold… Oh, My!

The most well-known local trapping expedition of this time was led by Jedidiah Smith. In 1828, Jedidiah, an already well known trapper, guided a team of twenty trappers and two hundred horses near here, coming up the Sacramento valley, then down the Trinity River and moving north to the Klamath, where he made his way down through the Yurok village of Kep'-el, crossing over Bald Hills and eventually making his way to the villages of O-men and O-men-hee-puer on the coast. In

---

[12] Pilot Rock is the large rock visible directly south of the Head and about a half mile out.
[13] Guess where…

fact, Jedidiah Smith State Park, in the redwoods, and the Smith River[14] are both named for him.

He wrote in his journals of how rough and rugged and miserable the terrain was around here, and how even then he tangled with some of the Indians, but that didn't do anything to discourage followers. One story says that when Jedidiah first spotted the ocean from the mountain tops, it still took him another ten days to actually reach the beaches due to the thick underbrush. Reading from his journal:

*"For a long time I had been travelling in a country where our utmost exertions would not enable us to travel more than 3 or 4 miles per day at most, where my horses were mangled by craggy rocks of the mountains over which they passed and suffered so much from hunger that I found myself under the necessity of stopping a while to rest them or run the risk of losing many of them if I should proceed."*

He also commented on the dense fog (that old zero-zero stuff) that settled in and wouldn't allow him to scout ahead for passage through the hills.

But in fact, his journals seemed to create interest, encouraging more and more white explorers, traders and trappers to enter the area. The fur trade included Pine Martens, Mink, Red Fox, Ringtail Cat, Bear, Sea Otter, Raccoon, Skunk,[15] Bobcat and any other fur bearing critter that could fetch a few dollars.

The discovery of gold in California in 1849 turned those explorers, traders and trappers into obsessed, fanatic and wild gold miners; along with settlers who wanted to claim the farmlands for themselves. Supply companies, which were where the real money was, began to look for coastal supply ports since

---

[14] The Smith is the largest river system in California that flows freely along its entire course – no damn dams.

[15] Yeah… I'd like to try on that skunk coat, there, and the matchin' hat, please.

the overland Sacramento Valley route that was being used at the time was slow and difficult and expensive as all get out.

Something like fifteen hundred and eighty gold mines, prospecting, and panning locations sprang up along the Klamath, Trinity and Smith Rivers, as well as the towns of Redding, Shasta, Whiskeytown, French Gulch, Weed, Orleans, Happy Camp and Crescent City. Gold mining production in this area of Northern California ended up being second only to the California Mother Lode itself.

Most people at the time believed that the Trinity River must run out and empty into Trinidad Bay. That was incorrect. Turns out that the Trinity is a branch of the Klamath River and they connect northeast of Trinidad, near the town of Weitchpec, which was a Yurok village at one time and is about twenty miles up the Klamath River.

In 1849, a small group of men led by Dr. Josiah Gregg decided that they would be the ones to find an overland route to the Pacific Ocean that would make supply to the mining areas easier. They left from Weaverville for the nearly one hundred and fifty mile hike to the sea with ten days' worth of supplies since they had been told it only takes about eight days to get here, but because of the rough and rugged and miserable terrain and the thick redwood forests, and because Gregg stopped frequently to measure the size of the trees, the expedition averaged only two miles a day. It seems that Jedidiah Smith wasn't exaggerating after all.

One of the party members, L.K. Wood, noted that *"The trip was one of constant and unmitigated toil, hardship, privation, and suffering."* Often there was no trail to follow. The party had to have two axemen ahead of the horses and mules to chop away brush and fallen logs just to keep moving. They fought ahead until finally they could only see a great stretch of snow on the steep mountain slopes in front of them. Oh, great! A number of times, they pondered whether or not to turn back, but Gregg urged them on.

In order to shorten the distance between themselves and the coast, they decided to climb the steepest part of the mountains in a straight line as much as possible until they finally reached the redwoods. The trail didn't get any easier, though, as the undergrowth in the redwood forest was dense and saturated with water. Several of the men thought of the redwoods as a 'prison' from which there might be no escape.

And starting out with only ten days' worth of supplies, it was no wonder that they nearly starved to death before finally making it to the coast where they at last stumbled out into this area,[16] coming out along Little River,[17] and wandering on up to Trinidad Bay. In fact, Gregg named the Head at Trinidad Bay 'Gregg's Point' before heading south and finally finding the 'Bay of Rezanov' on December 20, 1849. After a bit of rest, they did some mapping, stocked up on food and headed south to San Francisco to report their discovery. The name "Gregg's Point' didn't stick at Trinidad Bay, though. It was the Trinidad Head.

A quick story... Gregg was a scientist, not a gold seeker, which is why he spent so much time measuring the redwoods, which upset his companions to no end... they wanted to get a gold route open. There was frustration on both sides during the arduous trip. While doing even more scientific observations around the local rivers, his companions became frustrated and decided to leave him at one of the rivers, which made Gregg really angry. In fact, he was downright mad... which led to the naming of the Mad River. And nope... I didn't make that up.

Or... you can believe the story that Gregg fell in the river and lost his surveying equipment which made him mad, and so the river was named. Both stories show up in various records.

---

[16] Imagine the drive along Highway 299; only with no highway; you're on foot in a maze of steep canyons that twist and turn, plus the weather had to be against them as they left in November.

[17] South of Trinidad on 101, the river at the foot of the grade at the beginning of Clam Beach.

Maybe both stories are true... he got mad at his crew and then fell in the river, making him *really* mad... but then it would have been called the 'Furious River', so I don't know.

Then, in March of 1850, two ships, the *General Morgan* and the *Laura Virginia*, were sent from San Francisco to check out Gregg's report and mapping of the 'Bay of Rezanov', south of Trinidad Bay. This was what they had all been looking for.

They finally located the entrance and a small boat was launched with First Mate H.H. Buhne at the helm. After considerable difficulty with the huge breaker waves that rolled over the shifting sands of the bar crossing, their small boat finally managed to sail triumphantly into the harbor. The members of the *Laura Virginia* re-named the bay 'Humboldt Bay', in honor of Alexander von Humboldt, who was a famous German naturalist, even though von Humboldt had never been to this area. It's the second largest bay on California's coast. Buhne carefully mapped the entrance before leaving, so it remained 'found' this time.

Even with the current jetties, the bay entrance remains a tricky one to get in and out of. There's quite a list of ships that didn't make it and sank over the years... some resources reporting as many as one hundred and forty-two ships have been lost at the Humboldt Bay entrance since the 1800's. Eighty-one people drowned during bar crossings between 1853 and 1880 alone, including the captain of the brig *Crimea* who was washed overboard during a rough bar crossing in February of 1870. Well, stay out o' them bars!

Literally days after the *Laura Virginia's* 'discovery', the schooner, *James R. Whiting*, landed in the Trinidad/Big Lagoon area, in April of 1850. Captain Robert Parker, of the *Whiting*, was the first to lay out lines for a town on the slopes just west of the Tsurai Indian village. Parker was followed quickly by R.V. Warner, who arrived on schedule on the brig *Isabel* two days after Parker arrived. Warner laid out lines along Parker's for his own town, which he named Warnersville.[18] Parker noted that within the first three days of their 'town', they had elected an Alcalde[19]-who was pretty much a petty monarch with almost unlimited civil and judicial authority and was replaced by a Mayor in the next election - a second-Alcalde and sheriff with one hundred and four votes... and by the fifth day there were five hundred people who had claimed all the land by the bay in a process called 'pre-emption discovery'. Brush was cleared and pre-fab houses and tents and shanties sprung up like spring daffodils, including Parker's house, which was the first, Mr. Van Wyck's was second and Warner's was the third one finished.

By the end of June, even with people leaving for the gold fields, Trinidad – the name Warnersville didn't stick, it just wasn't catchy enough – had a population of three hundred with one hundred habitations including houses, tents, lean-to's and other shelters; all for the merchants, saloon keepers, hotels and boarding houses, stables, and blacksmiths who would supply everything needed by the miners heading out to the inland gold fields. Streets were named after schooners[20] and brigs and early settlers. North/South running streets were named after ships; Golinda, Mallory, Hector, Whiting, and East/West running streets were named after ship's captains; Parker, Edwards, Van Wyck. Golinda Street became the main street through town. That area has houses covering it now.[21]

Not long after getting the town started, R. V. Warner approached a local trapper and asked him if the coming winter was going to be a cold one. The trapper wasn't sure so he consulted a Tsurai village elder, who assured him that it would be wet and cold.

---

[18] Located along the bluffs above the current parking lots for the pier and Seascape restaurant. Where the town is now located would have been mostly dense, dark forested land back then.

[19] Alcalde is a Spanish term for mayor. I'm not sure why they didn't just elect a Mayor the first time around... they weren't Spanish.

[20] Look up schooner and brig in the Nautical Terms section of this book.

[21] I do not recommend a line of tourist cars parading through.

The trapper reported back to Warner that, indeed, it was going to be a wet and cold winter, so Warner told his folks to lay in a good supply of firewood. Warner worried about the time spent cutting firewood in relation to building the town, so he checked with the trapper once again. The trapper checked with the Tsurai elder who once again said, "It will be a wet and cold winter." The trapper told Warner that, yes, it was going to be very wet and very cold, so Warner had his folks redouble their effort at laying in wood.

Warner was a practical man and he didn't want to look foolish, so he checked with the trapper one more time just to be sure. The trapper again approached the Tsurai elder who told the trapper that this could be a one of the wettest and coldest winters in a long time. The trapper asked him how he could tell, and the elder said, "Haven't you noticed? The white men in that town are gathering firewood like crazy!"

There is no actual corroboration for that last story...

Captain Parker's wife started the first hotel in town, the Parker House, during 1850 since she and her husband had experience with the more famous Parker House, a well-known 'gambling house' on Kearny Street in San Francisco, before heading north. More hotels were to come, including Sangster's and Hanrahan's.

Where did all these prefab houses come from? When Parker and Warner landed, they had brought another ship, the *John Story*, with them carrying everything they would need to start a whole new life, including many of the prefab houses. What must the Yurok people have thought, watching these prefab jobs being set up so quickly? "Wow, they just don't build them like we used to."

Being the only viable harbor around at the time, the town of Trinidad continued to grow and become a town of prominence. In fact, Trinidad holds the distinction of being the County Seat of two different California counties. In 1850, California became a state and our first Governor, Peter Burnett, signed into law the creation of the state's original twenty-seven counties. They were as follows:[22]

Branciforte, Butte, Calaveras, Clusi, Contra Costa, El Dorado, Los Angeles, Marin, Mariposa, Mendocino, Monterey, Napa, Sacramento, San Diego, San Francisco, San Joaquin, San Luis Obispo, Santa Barbara, Santa Clara, Solano, Sutter, Trinity, Tuolumne, Yola, and Yuba.

Trinidad became the county seat of Trinity County until 1851, a fact that the residents of Union, to our south, disputed. Union, which is now called Arcata, was founded by L. K. Wood, who was one of Dr. Gregg's party as you may recall. When Klamath County was formed from the northern part of Trinity County, Trinidad then proudly became the county seat of Klamath County until 1854 when Klamath County was dissolved. By then, Humboldt County had been formed from the western part of Trinity County in 1853 and Union became a County Seat at last… until Eureka took away the title in 1856.

But Trinidad was still a County Seat first…so, you go, Trinidad!

Obviously, several other county names were changed by the legislature and other counties added throughout the late 1800's.

On a sad note, in 1850 newspapers noted the death of President Zachary Taylor. He died of a stomach ailment in July of that year and Millard Fillmore took over.

So; in Trinidad, outside contact was sparse in the early days. The first regular small express company started in 1851 when A. E. Raynes began a run from Trinidad to Bestville carrying letters, papers, gold dust and small packages. Bestville was a gold mining camp on the north fork of the Salmon River, near Sawyers Bar. Goods of any bulk were carried by the larger mule packers. Since Trinidad was at the head of all trails to the inland gold camps, twenty to thirty pack mule trains *per day* were going in and out of town, carrying two and a half tons of goods each. Pack trains charged three cents per pound with the average load running about three hundred pounds per mule. That works out

---

[22] From the California State Association of Counties.

to about nine dollars per mule to ship goods. The pack masters really had to know what they were doing to the balance the load on each mule so that they didn't tip over on unsteady ground.

Bestville was founded by Captain Francis Best who had come here on his own ship from New York when gold opened the area. He brought his brother-in-law, John Chapman with him. They came to mine for gold, but quickly discovered that there was more money in supplying the miners than digging for the gold, so they started one of the very first pack trains out of Trinidad. During a drunken argument in 1855, Chapman shot and killed Best and proceeded to take over the pack mule business until the bottom dropped out of gold mining and the packing business fell off in Trinidad. He then moved to Arcata and became an Indian Agent, using his mule train to transport Indians to the reservations.[23]

Other early packers were E. P. Rowe, Abisha Swain, Charles McDermit, Charles D. Moore, F. F. Marx, and E. W. Conner.

The intrepid packers blazed trails to the gold camps, although they mostly just followed old Indian trails that had been used for hundreds of years. But to be fair, they also carved out some new trails in the rugged country. One of the biggest hindrances to moving around was those darned, pesky redwood trees. They were so big and thick that you couldn't just chop them out of the way to build wagon trails or anything. It would take two weeks or more just to chop one down… and then what would you do with it? The darned things were huge! Plus the big tree canopies made it constantly dark in the forest with dangerous critters lurking about in there… like bears and panthers.[24] Back in the early days, there were grizzly bears here but they were hunted hard and by 1868, there weren't any more

---

[23] That story was told to me by Leslie Riecke, a descendant of Best.
[24] 'Panther' refers to a big cat, not necessarily just black ones. Mountain lions used to be referred to regularly as panthers around here. If you get confronted by one, stand tall and wave your arms to look as big as you can. Do not turn and run.

in Humboldt County. But we do have cute little black bears that can still tear you up. The panthers aren't so cute. They'll just shred you to pieces and then crunch your little bones. Oh, my!

That made sure footed pack mules the perfect answer for getting around. Pack trips often lasted several days one way, carrying food and equipment for the packers as well as their merchandise. And as relations with some of the local Indians were not good, every trip was a dangerous one. The long and difficult pack trips raised the already sky-high prices of supplies brought in by ship, but the miners were ready and willing to pay outrageous prices, so it was worth the risk for the packers.

One important pack trade route followed the beach from Trinidad to Crescent City, to our north. It wasn't all easy beach-going nature trails, though. There's some very rocky coastline between here and there. The trail was unending; climbing and dropping through steep, rocky ravines; in and out of brush and blackberry stickers; then hitting the beach for about six miles of sand that was loose and difficult to walk on and then you had to go clear around Big Lagoon... and that even *before* trying to cross the Klamath River.

At their peak, individual pack trains could have as many as a hundred mules trailing along. That's a lot of mules! The bell mare was always up front; usually a white mare with a small boy riding it, to lead the rest of the train. The boy was actually called the 'bellboy'. They could make twenty miles a day if the terrain wasn't too bad... which it often was. One mule was designated as the 'kitchen' and carried all the crew's camping gear. The crew usually consisted of four packers to load and unload the mules.

When ships landed in Trinidad Bay, the Indians always watched the proceedings carefully. Often mules were made to swim ashore. If a white mule was included, the Yuroks wanted to kill it as a white animal could be a sign of impending doom among their people... so that was a bit of cultural difference there among the folks.

Oh, and this isn't about an animal, but once, a load of food that included some horseradish washed ashore. One of the Tsurai villagers got into it and ate some of the horseradish, then stumbled home crying, "I am poisoned! I am poisoned!" I know just how he felt.

## You Have Mail

The Trinidad post office started in 1851 on Golinda Street, but the first Postmaster wasn't named until 1853. Mr. Lemuel Gilley stepped up and took that first position as Postmaster. Of course, there was still no way to transport mail other than the express company, so mail was irregular, to say the least... and we think it's slow today... and we complain that it costs forty-nine cents to mail a letter. In the mid-1800's, it cost around three dollars per letter for delivery once every three to four weeks!

The Pony Express hadn't been invented yet, and it never came up here anyway. There was no stage line because there were no roads. Walking, horses, and mule pack trains were the only way to move things like mail and supplies. We did finally start our own version of the Pony Express, though.

Charles Savage was the mail rider during the 1870's. His route was between Trinidad and Crescent City, and it wasn't an easy one. It mostly followed the pack routes, and you already know how difficult those were. When Charles retired from service, Dick Hayes took over and rode the route until wagon trails started being built and ferries ran across the rivers. That must have seemed like a milk run after what the riders had been through. Many a horse was lost to the surf over the years while making those early runs. I think it's safe to say that the more famous Pony Express had nothing on these guys. And you wonder why it cost so much to mail a letter...

## Gold Bluff... bluff...

About ten miles north of Trinidad, is a bluff known as 'Gold Bluff'.[25] The beach itself is about six miles long with the bluffs rising a hundred to five hundred feet above for several hundred feet along the beach. Remember that last part... the bluffs are several hundred feet long. Travelers using the trail between Trinidad and the mouth of the Klamath noticed some peculiar black sand exposed along the foot of the bluff, and with closer examination discovered that it was sprinkled with fine gold! At times, sections of the bluff would crumble and at higher tides, the crashing waves would carry off the coarser and lighter material down the beach back towards the sea, while the heavier black sand and gold would settle down at the foot of the bluff. It was basically the same action as a gold pan produces, only on a bigger scale.

In January of 1851, a couple of enterprising fellas, General John Wilson and John Collins, began working this black sand, staking claim to the bluff above. Seeing an opportunity beyond the small amounts of gold they were actually taking, the men went to San Francisco and sold shares in the property and... somehow... word got around that there was a *six mile long bluff*, with a beach of black sand that was yards wide and several feet deep and was one quarter to one half gold, that could just be shoveled up at low tide. Step right up, ladies and gentlemen, and take advantage of this once in a lifetime opportunity!

As you might expect, old hulks of any boat that floats off-loaded hundreds of investors and would-be millionaire miners at Trinidad. "We're gonna be rich, I tell you! Woo-hoo!"

Once they reached the bluffs and figured out that they'd been had, most of the angry investors and miners returned to San Francisco, but some of the more adventurous ones went on

---

[25] About three miles north of Orick, exit Hwy. 101 onto (gravel) Davison Road, which leads west eight miles to Gold Bluffs Beach. Be sure to visit Fern Canyon while you're there. There's a twenty-four foot vehicle length restriction, so be aware of that.

to the placer mines on the Klamath, between the junction of the Trinity River and the mouth of the Salmon River to try their luck. As it turned out, though, there was enough gold in and around the bluffs area to keep many of the miners here. The gold was just hard to process out of the sand, requiring a process involving quicksilver, which is another name for mercury.

The result of this overwhelming flood of miners was that, during the spring and summer of 1851, Trinidad was a 'lively little town'. In fact, during 1851 and 1852, the number of people going in and out of Trinidad at any one time is estimated to have swelled to over three thousand! There were tents pitched literally everywhere; on the beaches, on the bluffs, on the hills, and through the dales. I'm not sure who regulated the placement of privies[26] back then, but what a mess that would have been. Plus, you had to haul in water, and with that many hungry people coming and going, game hunting was soon a problem. But business boomed as those twenty to thirty pack trains continued to come and go to the inland mining towns every day and ships arrived daily with supplies and more eager people.

For the folks pouring into the area, ships' passage from San Francisco to Trinidad was thirty dollars per person, plus one dollar to be brought ashore, plus thirty dollars per ton for freight, plus another ten dollars to unload and bring that ashore. The ticket to bring up a mule by ship was forty dollars per mule… or you could buy a local mule for three hundred dollars. Most folks didn't have money for that. The tents that were pitched everywhere could be small single man tents or as big as twenty-five feet long and twelve feet wide to accommodate a family or to hold merchandise to be sold.

Landing a boat was difficult with the winds causing waves to crash on the Head and on shore and it was not unusual to lose one's goods in the water. At any given time, you could see a

---

[26] An outhouse… you know… the bathroom…

couple of barges, a couple of brigs and a schooner or two anchored and bobbing in the bay. Occasionally, an anchor would break and a barge or brig would end up crashing on the rocks. Newcomers were shocked and surprised to see the village of Indians right on the bay, with many of the women having tattooed chins,[27] and some of the older men naked as jaybirds!

Trinidad was *so* lively during those years that unruly trouble makers and jail prisoners would, on occasion, be left overnight on a rock in the harbor to consider their misdeeds. That rock is currently named 'Prisoner Rock'.[28] It was our own little Devil's Island.

In February of 1851, a young Swiss man, Jacob Christoph Brodbeck, looking to make his fortune in gold, landed here on the steamer *General Warren*, took a look around, and set himself up in business by renting an oven for fifty dollars a month to make money as a baker. He then used that money to purchase supplies before moving on to the inland gold fields in July of that same year. He noted that in June, six white people were killed by Indians on the Klamath River. A couple of days later, seven Indians were killed fourteen miles from Trinidad with one Indian being brought to town and shot there.[29]

But even with the 'Indian trouble', business went on. Trading for elk hides was booming at this point, too. The hides were highly prized to make gloves for the miners.

A couple of enterprising fellows named Marx and Nordheimer, who were Jewish merchants, owned the largest merchandise store in Trinidad by 1852. Quite a number of folks figured out that there was more money in supplying the miners than there was in searching for gold with the miners. At one time, there were at least twelve merchandise stores in Trinidad.

---

[27] Yurok men had lines tattooed on their arms to measure strings of dentalia shell money and the women had three lines referred to as '111' tattoos on their chins.
[28] From the corner of Trinity and Edwards Street, look into the bay. Prisoner Rock is two rocks close together off the pier a ways.
[29] Noted in a journal at the Humboldt County Historical Society.

Captain Merithew opened a store in 1854. The 'Old Brick Store' was another, built on Golinda Street in 1851 or '52 with locally made bricks, possibly from a site on Mill Creek. This store had iron bars on the windows to keep raiding Indians out and the occasional prisoner in, as the building was also used as a jail from time to time. Brothers Josiah and Philetus Bell operated the old Brick Store starting about 1870 and it later became the Trinidad Mill Company store. In 1895, Tommy Tighe had a store near Hanrahan's Hotel and Saloon. Sangster's had a tobacco shop nearby, too. But that's jumping ahead of my story.

Downtown Trinidad – Old Brick Store behind the wagon

About the raiding Indians; it wasn't always the local Yuroks... in fact, it was almost never the local Tsurai. Other tribes often raided each other as well as hitting back at the whites. The Chilulas seemed to be ones always spoiling for a fight with somebody even before the white men showed up. In fact, the Tsurai had actually asked Bodega y Quadra to stay and help them fight other coastal Indians back in 1775. But keep in mind that no one actually asked the Yuroks or any of the Indians if they wanted to give up their lands and customs once the whites did arrive. They were fighting to keep what was theirs. 'Indian attacks' were commonplace and often deadly —as were attacks by the whites on Indians; not so much in town where there so many concentrated white men, but for the trappers and miners... and for the Yuroks... it could a dangerous and violent time to move about Yurok country.

And while violence certainly took its toll, diseases that the white men brought with them were the bigger killer. In 1852, a measles epidemic struck the upper Klamath and killed nearly half the Indians along the river. Their 'cure' of spending time in a sweathouse then plunging themselves in the icy Klamath River was of no help with the disease. The Indians had never been exposed to most of the white men's diseases. Across the country, disease killed more Indians than any fighting with the whites did.

Smallpox, diphtheria, cholera and even influenza were mostly unknown in this area until the whites brought them in. And most Indian tribes believed that disease only entered the body if one was not 'protected by the spirits'. They had no immunity or ideas how to fight it.

## Hey, Look at Them Big Trees

Lumbering started in this area in 1850, but, surprisingly, several years went by before any real attention was paid to the redwoods as anything but a nuisance. Remember, these trees, *Sequoia sempervirens*, are the tallest and one of the most massive tree species on Earth, reaching nearly four hundred feet tall and thirty feet in diameter at chest high and living for two thousand years. The bark is thick and fire resistant. The root system is surprisingly shallow, but spreads out massively, intertwining with other trees. The first lumbermen in this area were from the northeast, and knew how to log and manufacture the pine, spruce, and fir from back east for use in the building trades, but because their mills weren't equipped to handle the huge redwood logs found here, and being unfamiliar with its value for lumber, no redwood was shipped from Humboldt Bay until 1854!

The first sawmill on Humboldt Bay was the *Papoose;* started up in the summer of 1850 by a couple of enterprising young men, Martin White and James Eddy. Remember, the first successful mapping of the bay was just a few months earlier in this same year. White and Eddy hired a Canadian, William Carson, to supply them with logs. Carson and Jerry Whitmore fell the first tree - yes, fallers fell a tree, you can look it up - they fell the first tree for commercial purposes in what was to become Humboldt County. Carson also brought in the first ox teams used in local logging.

The Papoose mill failed within the year. But their very first shipment of lumber was loaded aboard the *James H. Whiting* – the same ship that had left the settlers who founded Trinidad. Unfortunately, the *Whiting* was lost in Noyo Harbor in Mendocino County with the loss of seven lives in November 1865 during a severe storm.

But there's another story about the first *successful* lumber mill in Humboldt County:

James Ryan bought the steamer *Santa Clara* in 1852 and loaded it with sawmill machinery in San Francisco to take up the coast to his partner James Duff. As they were making the dangerous bar crossing at the entrance to Humboldt Bay, some of the machinery was washed overboard... a disaster! Except that Ryan thought about it, then had the *Santa Clara* anchored, and had a crew dig a slipway; which is a sloped ramp next to the water. Then they built up a full head of steam and the ship was driven hard aground on the slipway.

Ryan figured that the ship's engines could be used to power a sawmill that he and Duff could build right there on the beach. Within a short time, they were sawing several thousand board feet[30] of spruce, fir, and pine a day. In June, they loaded their first shipment on the *John Clifford*. Heading across the dangerous bar crossing, the ship grounded and was pounded to pieces. Several days later, they tried again with the *Cornwallis*, only to see a repeat of the *Clifford*. Then they recruited Hans H. Buhne - who had brought that launch from the *Laura Virginia* into Humboldt Bay - to take out a third shipment. On July 4, 1852, the *Home* hoisted anchor and made sail, but was driven ashore on the south spit. Oh, come on!

And, as if that wasn't enough, later on, their mill was destroyed by fire. Ryan and Duff persisted, though, and continued on in business. Success!

In 1851, Baron Karl von Loeffelholtz came to America from Germany and spent eight thousand dollars to build a sawmill just south of Trinidad. His name was Americanized to Luffenholtz, which is the name we recognize. The town was located well up on the plateau way above the beach,[31] but the mill itself was on (now) Luffenholtz Creek, just sixty or eighty feet above the high water mark off the beach below.

In 1852/'53, the mill was rented by Bryon March who, with a partner named William Deming, had helped build Loeffelholtz's mill. He operated it until he and Deming built their own mill just north of Trinidad in 1853. A Mr. Krutschmitt then took over the Loeffelholtz lease, but unfortunately for Krutschmitt, the mill was totally destroyed by flooding and heavy seas — what they call a *freshet* - in an 1854 storm. It was not rebuilt and in 1856 Loeffelholtz returned to Germany, not quite the rich man he had hoped to become. Of course, not getting rich was the case for many immigrants.

---

[30] A board foot is a piece of lumber measuring one foot by one foot by one inch thick. That's different from a cubic foot which is one foot by one foot by one foot.

[31] The town was about where Westhaven Drive and Old Wagon Road intersect.

March and Deming opened their mill on the bluffs above what is now Trinidad State Beach.[32] The mill was water powered, using Mill Creek as the water source and it overlooked the ocean with incredible views of Flatiron Rock – the big flat rock just offshore - and Pewetole (Pee-weh-toll-ee) Island, which is the one all covered with Sitka Spruce. Of course, the mill workers didn't have time to sightsee. They had to pay close attention to their work just to keep all their fingers.

For example; one day, while greasing the gears and all the metal parts in one of the shingle mills, one of the mill workers saw out of the corner of his eye a chip of wood dropping in the grease as he poured it on some moving gears. Realizing that the chip was big enough to jam up the gears, and without really thinking about it, he grabbed at the chip and got his right thumb and a couple of fingers caught in the moving parts. Ouch![33] When he managed to get his hand free, his thumb, index finger and middle finger had been torn off at the knuckles. Just like that.

Back in 1853, there was one… as in, one… doctor between Crescent City and Mendocino. He was a French doctor named Monsieur Gras, and whatever he charged for a house call, it wasn't enough. And however good he was, he couldn't have saved the man's fingers anyway.

By 1875, Trinidad was being served by Dr. Cabaniss of Eureka. He noted that in November of that year;

*"It was astonishing the number of accidents that have happened during the past month, and invariably they occurred among the working class. We now have in good working order the 'Workingman's Protective Association', and we should think that those who are liable to have an arm, hand, or leg taken off at any moment, while working in the mills or logging claims, would take*

---

[32] Turn right on Stagecoach Road from town and you'll see the sign for the State Beach parking lot.
[33] I'm guessing he used more colorful and descriptive words.

*advantage of this opportunity and have their names enrolled immediately upon the books of this organization."*

But about the mills...

The story about Deming and March's mill goes two ways; that they started a new mill or that they moved the Loeffelholtz mill to their new location. Possibly it was both... possibly they started a new mill using machinery from the Loeffelholtz mill. There's no confirmation either way, so don't quote me.

But anyway, even with these mills being built around town, no one was logging or milling any redwood yet.

1854; William Carson – the fella who was a faller who fell trees - purchased the Muley Mill in Eureka; it was a small mill capable of producing only five thousand board feet of lumber a day and was operated by three or four men. However, Carson figured out that by selecting smaller redwood logs, and not handling anything larger than five feet in diameter, he was able to ship twenty thousand board feet of redwood lumber to San Francisco aboard the two-masted ship *Tigress*. It was the first shipment of redwood from the area. A house takes about fifteen or sixteen thousand board feet of lumber to build, so they shipped enough wood for one house and a comfortable sized privy. And that's back when a 2 X 4 was actually a full two inches by four inches!

Sawmills initially used a single blade moved up and down by a crank, then a longer sash saw, then the sash-gang saw which had two or more saws in the sash cutting at the same time. Saws to cut redwood had to be made stronger and more durable than saws used in standard mills. Fast circular saws, invented locally, replaced the reciprocating blade saws. Then came the double circular saw. Blade sizes increased from twelve inches to eventually as much as seventy-two inches. Double circular saws were replaced by newly invented Third Saws where four saws worked in tandem to cut one even larger log, and finally the first band saw on the Pacific Coast was used here on the North Coast. Mills were often located on creeks so they could use the water to power the equipment. That's why Trinidad has Mill Creek, and Luffenholtz Creek, and McConnaha Creek. Steam boilers eventually replaced water power.

The mills didn't use a water wheel like those seen on the sides of paddle wheel boats. They used what would today be called a turbine, whose wooden or metal teeth mesh with the iron teeth of the gears that lead to the drive of the saw. It's very technical.

But back to my story... in San Francisco the redwood was a hit, and because of its rot-resistance, the lumber was sold at premium prices. Score one for William Carson. With this success, the lumbermen really ripped into the redwood forests.

By the end of 1854 there were nine more mills operating around Humboldt Bay. Within thirty years the North Coast had four hundred mills cutting some of the largest trees in the world. As the gold rush slowed, Trinidad Bay, like most lagoons, sloughs and streams along the Redwood Coast, became home to multiple sawmills.

To aid the many ships now hauling lumber to market, a lighthouse was proposed for the ocean-facing side of the Trinidad Head in 1854. Forty-two acres were purchased for a light station on the southern portion of the Head, but work on the project didn't actually begin for nearly twenty years.

The first lighthouse in Humboldt Bay was located on the northern entrance to the bay in 1856. It served as both a coastal and a harbor light. However, since it was prone to flooding and socked in by fog most of the time, it was relocated in 1892 to Table Bluff, four miles south of the entrance to the bay and built one hundred and sixty-five feet high. Much better!

## Indian Trouble... or was it White Man trouble?

Relations with the local Indians hadn't improved any with the lumbermen now out scouring the woods for trees as well as the miners still tearing up the ground like they owned it.

Early in 1853, the army sent three companies of troops to the area under Colonel Buchanan, with one of the companies commanded by a young Capt. Ulysses S. Grant, to 'assist with conflict resolution'. People expected that the troops would be stationed in the heart of the Indian country around the Trinity and Klamath Rivers, but the officer in charge took a look around, carefully evaluated the situation and decided that he preferred a pleasant site overlooking Humboldt Bay to the rugged mountain region for his headquarters, and he founded Fort Humboldt... not exactly in the thick of it all.

As for Grant, he visited Trinidad occasionally proclaiming it, "A place I used to visit". Actually, Grant only stayed for about six months before resigning his commission and leaving the area.

The white men continued to encroach on ceremonial lands and attacking villages and villagers, and taking game that was the food of the Indians. In retaliation, the Indians raided livestock and attacked their attackers. It was a time of raids and counter-raids that led to skirmishes and even to war.

U.S. Army in the Redwoods

## What Gold?

So, the lumber business was picking up, but then the gold mining boom went bust... just like that! One day it's there...

By 1854, the population of Trinidad had fallen to one hundred and four people as the gold mines petered out and the town of Union finished their wharf in 1855, making it a much easier place to off-load and load lumber cargo ships... even with the dangerous bar crossing out of Humboldt Bay. They even had a railroad/tram two miles long using a horse as the locomotive.

Trinidad had no wharf and remained a dangerous and difficult place for cargo ships until 1859, when Charles B. Ryder completed work on the Trinidad wharf which was located on the Head.[34] Prior to the wharf, loading ships was done by means of heavy cables extending from shore out into the bay and attached to a buoy. The ship to be loaded was attached to other buoys with the crew picking up the cable and making it fast to one of the ship's masts. The cable was then drawn taut and the lumber, which was in sling loads on a trolley, was hauled aboard from shore. "Heave ho! Look lively, there, men!"

Many parts of the town fell into disrepair with the population drain caused by the loss of the gold mining trade. In fact, by 1854 only ten of the original one hundred houses in Trinidad were occupied. But those who remained were determined to take full advantage of what was left. Marx and Nordheimer hung in there with their store, and Captain Merithew's store stayed open, but that was about it. Another merchant named Rotenheimer had to close his store and leave town.

By this time, grist and flour mills had been established along Yeager Creek, the Mad River, and Eureka, however shanties and block houses south of Little River were now deserted since farming and ranching (where vegetables, fruit crops, grains and

---

[34] You can still see remains from the old wharf along the Head from the Trinidad pier.

livestock made up the local agriculture community) couldn't take the costs for labor as wages were three to five dollars per day. Things picked up by 1875 though, when one hundred and twenty-seven thousand pounds of butter were shipped from Humboldt County... but that was mostly from the Ferndale area, to our south.

Elk meat sold for twenty-five to thirty cents per pound in those days. Coffee that sold for forty dollars per pound two years earlier now went for closer to five dollars a pound. The price of flour also plummeted as did prices of everything.

When Ryder completed work on his wharf in 1859, it cost him eight thousand dollars to build. In order to facilitate getting lumber to his wharf from Deming and March's mill on the bluffs, Ryder also dug a tunnel[35] through Trinidad Head. The tunnel had wooden narrow gauge rails through it so the mule drawn lumber cars could bring wood right to the wharf. But even the wharf didn't make it much easier to load ships. Because of the wharf's location right against the Head, it was still a dangerous proposition to load and unload the steamers and sailing ships because they rolled and tossed with the action of waves crashing against the Head and wharf while cranes attempted to hoist lumber aboard the bouncing vessels. Not an easy task!

In January of 1869, a storm demolished the wharf and most of the wharf road anyway. Hey, at least it wasn't fire! Keep reading... you'll see.

## Sawmills to the Rescue

Partners Smith and Daugherty built a new shingle mill in Trinidad in 1869 just south of town on the other Mill Creek, which created a number of jobs. That Mill Creek was later

---

[35] You can't see the tunnel. It was a hazard from the beginning and closed up in 1913. The entrance to the tunnel was about where the gate is on the road to the lighthouse today.

renamed McConnaha[36] Creek. In fact, they quickly became the largest mill in Trinidad before selling out to the Hooper Brothers from San Francisco in 1875.

As a matter of reference, our old friend, Ulysses S. Grant, who had been stationed at Fort Humboldt and had occasionally visited Trinidad many years earlier, and who had some success in the Civil War, had risen to become President of the U.S. by this time. No one necessarily credits his visits here with his success, though.

In 1875, the Hooper Brothers also bought out Deming and March and consolidated that mill with the one they bought from Smith and Daugherty, forming the Trinidad Mill Company and hiring Josiah Bell to be their superintendent. Josiah had mill experience from his days in Port Orford, Oregon where he built one of the early mills up there. They converted Deming and March's mill from water power to steam power, which was a major technological improvement at that time. Steam boilers were easily and very cheaply powered by using scrap wood left from the milling operations and there was enough wood around to last a lifetime... heck, several lifetimes! They'd probably never run out of wood...

Once, in the 1870's, a boiler exploded in the mill on Mill Creek. The boiler blew clear out of the mill and landed on the bank across the ravine in back of the mill and stuck in the mud. An Indian worker had been handling slabs near the boiler and was also blown out of the mill, but was unharmed. When he returned to the scene a week later, he refused to go in the mill, saying, "White man's smoke house no good!" He never returned... not sure I can blame him.

Stories say that the Hooper's also owned a shingle mill, but after a lot of research, I still don't know where it was... unless it was part of the main sawmill.

I also suspect that there were a lot of really small shingle mills spread hither and yon throughout the woods, but there

---

[36] That's pronounced "Mc-Conna-hay."

aren't any records of them... and many of them most likely didn't last very long and no one kept track of them anyway. Shingle mills were a lot easier to set up than a large sawmill, but they would have had trouble securing trees and shipping could be a costly venture for the small-timers.

The mill was off to the center-left of the picture, down on the bluff. You can see the trestle that ran from the mill to the wharf.

The consolidated mill operation was a big success and by 1881, the brothers owned ten thousand acres of first-class redwood timber land. They ran their own four mile rail line between their logging operations in the woods and the mill at a cost of fifteen thousand dollars per mile. Another half mile tramway from the mill to the Trinidad wharf ran mostly over a trestle that was sixty feet high for the most part... except for the part that ran through the Trinidad Head tunnel. The consolidated mill company eventually processed sixty to seventy thousand board feet of lumber per day, plus they had the shingle mill that ran about another thirty thousand board feet per day. They employed a good two hundred men in the woods and in their mills… which was just about the entire population of Trinidad.

In 1878, as many as eighteen ships per day were coming in and out of Trinidad Bay bringing supplies in and taking lumber out.

Josiah Bell remained the superintendent of the Trinidad Mill Company until 1881 when the mill was sold to a syndicate of Scottish investors, the California Redwood Company.

1881 is also when the Earp brothers had their thirty second shootout with the Clanton's at the OK Corral in Tombstone, Arizona. It was a busy year all around.

After leaving the mill, Josiah moved to Eureka where he finished out his career as director and vice-president of the Humboldt County Bank as well as secretary and superintendent of the Elk River railroad. He died in August of 1920.

By 1886, though, the California Redwood Company had gotten themselves in a bit of trouble with the government. In fact, The California Redwood Company was forced to close all of their lumber operations in 1886 when government investigations revealed fraudulent dealings in acquisition of much of their timberland.

That was a big blow to the community and local government just about collapsed with the town. Things were quiet in Trinidad until a fire destroyed the old Deming/March portion of the mill buildings later in 1886. There was no point in rebuilding.

Philetus Bell – everyone called him 'Leet' - and a partner named Hansen opened another shingle mill by the bay in 1892 when business picked up a bit. They ran three shingle machines, producing about one hundred and eighty thousand shingles in a single ten hour shift. Charlie Blank had the job of moving carts of shingles to the wharf to be loaded on ships. He used a little old mule to pull the carts across the trestle until they reached the tunnel through the Head, where Charlie would unhook the mule and let gravity take the carts the rest of the way down to the wharf. The mule followed along and by the time Charlie had the carts unloaded, the little old mule would catch up to them and be ready to pull everything back up to the mill.

That mill lasted until 1903. Philetus still had the general merchandise store during this time, too. After his mill years, Leet went on to become the Assessor of Humboldt County. He died in 1937.

The shingle mills produced shingles and shakes, fence posts, pickets and railroad ties for the most part. They didn't produce lumber boards as the bigger mills did. What's the difference between shingles and shakes? Shingles are sawn from a block, also called a 'bolt' of wood, while shakes are split off by machine or using a mallet and froe.[37] Sawn or split... that's the difference. There's a little difference in the shape and thickness, too.

The shingle mills were cheaper to set up than a full sawmill and demand was high, so there were a bunch of them all over the county and they came and went. It's hard to pin down exactly when and where some of them were. But with four hundred mills in the area over the years, guys could generally get a job if they wanted one.

Most of the mills back then tried to take care of their men and often, when a man became too old to work in the mill, he would be kept on to run a hand powered contraption to make pickets for fencing or some other menial job so he could still make a living. Social security was still a ways off.

Wages ran somewhat like this:

- Common Yard Hands made thirty to sixty dollars per month.
- Helpers in the mill made thirty to fifty dollars a month.
- Edgers and Trimmers made fifty to eighty-five dollars.
- Sawyers and Filers made eighty-five to one hundred dollars.

---

[37] Yes, I know... shingles are a bad rash and shakes are thick ice cream drinks.

- Engineers and machinists made a hundred to one hundred and twenty-five dollars.

## Patrick's Point

Just five miles north of Trinidad proper, there's a pleasant tree and meadow covered headland that sticks out into the ocean. An explorer and trader named Patrick Beegan, who was an Irish immigrant from the Mississippi Valley, wandered onto the headland area in 1851 and after finding wild potatoes, which were his favorite food from the old homeland, "Old Patrick", as he became known to the residents of Trinidad, decided to stop and file a claim to the headland. He built a trading post which did all right for a while, but when the access point for miners and their supplies shifted from Trinidad to Union – which is now Arcata - Beegan abandoned his plan and the property.

Old Patrick was apparently not a particularly nice man. He drank excessively, hated the Indians and was ultimately killed by the Chilulas in the 1860s.

Now, there's another story that says Patrick McLaughlin, a squatter who arrived later in the 1870s, squatted on the point to plant the first apple trees around here, and the point was named for him. McLaughlin had his own funny ways including a distrust of banks, preferring to bury his money beneath the apple trees.[38]

So which was it? Patrick Beegan had been gone some thirty years before the name 'Patrick' was assigned to the area, but his claim to the land was first recorded in the Trinidad Record Book on January 13, 1851. The first official mention of Patrick's Point on the Humboldt County map was in 1886. You can decide who the park is named for.

In any case, between 1875 and 1925, 'Patrick's Ranch' was nearly wiped out as the forest was heavily logged, cleared and burned in order to graze sheep and cattle and to plant hay and

---

[38] You can look, but don't go digging.

potato crops and apple orchards. Efforts to protect the area led to the establishment of Patrick's Point as a state park, eventually covering an area of four hundred and twenty acres.[39]

In the 1880's sulfur ore was found near Abalone Point.[40] Chinese laborers were used to mine for the ore until they were banned from the county in 1885. There wasn't enough ore to make a mine of it anyway. In February of 1885, Eureka's entire Chinese population of three hundred men and twenty women were expelled after a gunfight between rival Chinese gangs resulted in the wounding of a twelve year-old boy and the death of fifty-six year old David Kendall, a Eureka City Councilman. Don't be shootin' them politicians. After the shooting, an angry mob of six hundred Eureka residents met and informed the Chinese that they were no longer wanted in Eureka and would be hanged if they were to stay in town longer than three p.m. the next day. Two loaded steamships left the next morning for San Francisco. Within a short period of time, other towns throughout the county followed suit since, besides cultural differences, it was felt that the Chinese were unfairly taking jobs from hard working folks during the harsh winter job slowdown.

But anyway, neither one of the Patricks' was the first in the area by a long shot. Yurok activity has been dated back to 1310 A.D. on the point where it was an intertribal trading and spiritual questing area. The Yuroks believed that it was the final abode of all the primordial underworld spirits, including Thunder, Earthquakes, and the Eleven Porpoise Brothers.

## Can I Have an Amen to That?

Speaking of spiritual things, logging and mill work was a dangerous job in those early days. It was hard work with long hours… so lumbermen became staunch recreational drinkers,

---

[39] Five miles north of Trinidad on Highway 101, look for the signs for Patrick's Point State Park.
[40] In Patrick's Point State Park.

which may have led in 1875 to the first temperance organization, the 'Reformed Drunkards', being formed in Trinidad. The 'Sons of Temperance' followed and eventually became the 'Good Templars', a popular civic organization. The Holy Trinity Catholic Church[41] was established in Trinidad in 1873, too, so there were places that drunkards could go for help if they wanted it. The Catholic Church is the oldest standing building still in town. The lighthouse is older, but it's not in town... it's way up on the Head.

And speaking of drinking, John Flaherty opened a new saloon and billiard room in 1870. There were seven saloons in town in 1870, and two remained by 1879. That's temperance for you!

Gambling saloons were the first buildings to get all gussied up; even when in shake buildings with canvas walls, an attempt was made to 'add ornamentation, to render them attractive and inviting to the eye contrasting with the general crudeness of their surroundings'. On the other hand, church organizations were slow in forming. They came next after the secret societies... like the Masons... shhhhh...

Robert Phillips owned the largest saloon in Trinidad in 1880. It was conveniently placed right across the street from the Occidental Hotel. Phillips sold his saloon to Mike Hanrahan in 1891. He (Phillips) died in 1894 and is buried in the Trinidad cemetery.

As I mentioned, the Templars became a popular civic group. You may have noticed the photographs in this book... most of them were taken by A.W. (Gus) Ericson who took up photography in about 1879 and became quite famous for his pictures. From 1869 to 1876 he lived in Trinidad while working in the Hooper Brothers lumbering enterprise and then in a retail store. Mr. Erickson was also very active in the Templars during his Trinidad years. He also operated the first telegraph station in Trinidad from the Old Brick Store. This was a busy man!

---

[41] At the corner of Parker and Hector Streets.

## Now that's Entertainment!

One of the more popular establishments in Trinidad from 1876 to 1885 was that of Miss Cockeyed Florence. Yeah... you can see where this is going, can't you. Cockeyed Florence was a 'soiled dove' who ran a house of ill-repute[42] that catered to the miners and trappers and woodsmen who stopped by her place on their way to the docks. It could get lonely out at sea or trampling around the forests or working those gold diggings with nothing but other guys around all the time. Trinidad had a number of gambling and drinking establishments as well as houses of prostitution over the years. Florence's was just one of the more popular ones.

Florence died in 1885, and legend says that while she died anything but a pauper, the good folks of Trinidad didn't quite want her buried in the same cemetery as the proper folks, so she was buried in the road of the cemetery. Supposedly it's unmarked, but you can drive over and say hi.[43]

Other entertainments included 'traveling shows' with professional performers. These were classier than the 'medicine shows' that hit the gold camps just to fleece customers.

In 1870, Charles Vincent came to town with a show called, 'Blondes, Brunettes, and Comedians'.

Then Nickerson's Troupe came to town in 1871 and put on several shows that played to rave reviews:

*"We cannot speak too complimentary as the overpacked house last night testified. In fact, no such combination of genuine and varied talent ever visited Humboldt County before, and we doubt if elsewhere in the State. Mlle. Forrestelle advertised as the 'Wonder Woman' is possibly spare in this issue to explain the many wonders she accomplishes. She is a grand contortionist."*

---

[42] It was in a house next to where the Windan Sea gift shop is now. The gift shop was an old barn at the foot of View Street and Main at that time.
[43] Drive over... she's buried in the road... I tell you, I'm hilarious! I'll be here all week.

In 1876, Belasco and Troupe came in on horseback with sets and props and everything from San Francisco and put on a fine show called 'The Black Hand' for the folks at the ballroom on the third floor of the Occidental Hotel. It was a grand old time.

## Grave Matters

Speaking of Florence and the Trinidad Cemetery, the oldest grave marked there is from 1862. One headstone reads; 'Elizabeth Jane Taylor, born April 8, 1852, Died August 23, 1866 – 14 years old, a wife and homemaker'. It's believed that she died bearing her first child. Life was hard back then.

If you look closely at a lot of the older headstones, it seems that everybody died on the twenty-third of whatever month. I'm not sure why that is.

Somewhere in the graveyard – records have been lost so no one knows just where – is a common grave for thirty-seven bodies recovered from the wreck of the *Brother Jonathon*. The *Brother Jonathon* sank off the Crescent City coast on July 30, 1865 during a massive storm. The ship was carrying two hundred and forty-four passengers and crew, along with a large shipment of gold.[44] They were trying to make the safety of the port in Crescent City, but hit some rocks, tearing a hole in the hull. Only nineteen people survived, making it the deadliest shipwreck up to that time on the Pacific Coast of the United States. No one knows for sure why so many victims were buried all the way down here in Trinidad.

This wreck had a lot to do with the establishment of the Trinidad lighthouse and other lighthouses on the north coast.

Safety First! ... or at least in the top three.

There's another famous headstone there for a shingle mill owner, Edward Schnaubelt, but I'll dig into that later.

---

[44] Somebody already beat you to it. The gold has been recovered.

## Schools

Trinidad's first school was built in 1870. The Hooper Brothers donated a plot of land near the cemetery[45] for the school building, and Harry Gastman constructed a sturdy school house for the sum of two hundred and twenty dollars in gold. Mr. C.R. Saunders taught there from 1870 to 1874. He was followed by Mr. Dickson who taught from 1874 to 1881.

In 1890, the school had thirty-five students with Mr. Edgerton as the teacher.

Sixth grade kids were tested on things like; A wagon box is two feet deep, ten feet long, and three feet wide. How many bushels of wheat will it hold? And; Give rules for the principal marks of Punctuation. Ummmmm... what?

Mr. Shirley[46] Hannah, who was paid one hundred dollars a month for ten months of the year, was the teacher in 1914 when a couple of disgruntled students burned the building to the ground. The building was sturdy, but not fireproof. I'm guessing that they got suspended... or whupped... or both. They could do that back then.

I'm not sure if they were sixth grade students afraid of one of those tests or not.

The school was rebuilt near the present school location on Trinity Street and burned again in 1949.

## Fish

Salmon fisheries sprang up along the Eel River as early as 1851, and within seven years two thousand barrels of cured fish and fifty thousand pounds of smoked salmon were processed and shipped out of Humboldt Bay annually from processing plants on Eureka's wharf.

---

[45] A 'plot' of land near the cemetery... get it?
[46] Shirley was a man's name in those days.

Bottom fish trawlers also became active along the North Coast and specifically in the Eureka area by 1929, where they delivered their catch for shipment to larger population centers by rail. Also around that time several seafood companies - many of which originated in San Francisco - began doing business with fishermen along the North Coast.

Nontribal fisheries for Coho and Chinook salmon were locally active since the mid-1800's, too. The official ocean salmon fishery, begun in Monterey in the late 1880's, reached the North Coast by the 1920's and a commercial salmon fleet was active in Trinidad Bay by the late '20's. This 'mosquito fleet'[47] grew to as many as four hundred boats by the 1960's.

Primarily, fishermen fish for Dungeness crab using crab pots, hook and line is used for various bottom fish such as rockfish and lingcod and halibut, and trolling[48] is done for salmon.

Oh, this is sort out of place but it's about fish... sort of... Humboldt County ranks Number One in shark attacks[49] statewide, according to statistics from the Florida Museum of National History, despite the area's small population in comparison to the surfing hotspots in Southern California.

The organization's 2007 International Shark Attack File listed Humboldt at Number One in attacks within the last twenty years. We'd like to thank the members of the academy for this award...

## Ship Building

In 1854 the first of many ships built in Eureka was launched, setting off an industry that spanned decades. Allen & Co. built the first steamer on Humboldt Bay. The Eureka &

---

[47] Individually owned boats.
[48] Trolling means to draw several baited lines through the water, generally by boat.
[49] Yes, we have Great Whites.

Union Transportation Company was also founded about then using the Steamer *Glide* to serve Eureka and Arcata commerce on Humboldt Bay.

It was soon reported that "There are five ship-yards in the vicinity of Eureka. Oregon pine,[50] as it is called, is very valuable for ship-building, preferred indeed, to the article found in higher latitudes. The material is here in abundance for conducting this business extensively." And certainly there were plenty of sawmills in the area to provide the shipbuilders with all the wood they could possibly use.

In 1873, Danish ship builder, Hans Bendixson, bought the former Fay brothers shipyard in Fairhaven on the north peninsula of the bay. The Bendixson shipyards alone produced one hundred and twenty ships, both sail and steam powered, on Humboldt Bay. The shipyard changed hands several times before being purchased by James Rolf in 1917. Rolf prospered because of World War I, but the shipyard closed after the war. Ship building revived briefly during World War II when the Chicago Bridge and Iron Works built floating dry docks at the foot of Washington Street in Eureka... but that's all closed up now, too.

By the 1880s, long wharves were built along Humboldt Bay for the lumber shipments and shipbuilding was a key part of the process. Shipping reached about six hundred vessels a year by 1881.

Of course, the villagers in Tsurai had been building their quality boats since the 1100's... or whenever.

## Indian Wars

Through the last half of the 1800's the relationship between the Yuroks and settlers went steadily downhill as more and more settlers moved into the area, showing their hostility towards the Indian people. Remember that the miners, trappers

---

[50] 'Oregon pine' is really Douglas fir.

and settlers brought a long tradition of prejudice against Indians and their way of life with them. Most new Americans believed that it was their right and destiny to settle and civilize any territory that was inhabited by 'primitive savages'.

And the settlers were relentless in their pursuit of lumber and gold. They 'boldly went where no man had gone before', encountering camps of Indian people, which led to hostility from both sides, which led to bloodshed and loss of life on both sides. The result was the destruction of villages which left the culture of the natives severely damaged. By the end of the gold rush era, it's estimated that at least seventy-five percent of the Yurok people had died due to massacres and disease.

In 1858, a war with the Indians– the Bald Hills War – broke out and lasted until 1864. The war involved the Red Cap Indians, who were a group made up of several local tribes unhappy about having their lands stolen and being punished for objecting to the practice. Enough was enough. In 1855 they revolted against the settlers and were successful in stopping new settlements for a short time. Federal troops were sent in to regain control of the area, and were engaged in a full scale fight by 1858, but then they got recalled in 1861 to go fight in the American Civil War, so the California Militia was dispatched to Fort Humboldt in Eureka. From July to October 1863, California Volunteers were stationed in Trinidad to protect it and the coast road from Indian raids. The overall war was fought within the boundaries of Mendocino, Trinity, Humboldt, Klamath, and Del Norte counties.

The Federal Government established the Yurok Reservation, which was considerably smaller than the Yurok original ancestral territory, in 1855 under the direction of President Franklin Pierce, and immediately confined the Indians to the area. Fortunately, the Reservation boundaries included a portion of the Yurok's original territory including most of their villages, so the Yurok people were not entirely forcibly removed from their traditional homelands; although when the army garrison Fort Ter-Wer was established in 1857 six miles from the mouth of the Klamath River, many Yurok families were relocated and forced to learn farming and the English language.

**Indian Island Massacre**

On February 26, 1860, at Tuluwat on what is now called 'Indian Island' in Humboldt Bay, more than eighty elderly men, women and children, including babies, were murdered during a Wiyot World Renewal Ceremony by a mob of whites with axes, knives, and guns in what is known as the 'Indian Island Massacre'. The actual number of those killed is in dispute with some saying the number was as high as two hundred people killed on the island. Bret Harte, who was living in Arcata at the time, published a detailed account condemning the event, writing:

*"A more shocking and revolting spectacle never was exhibited to the eyes of a Christian and civilized people. Old women wrinkled and decrepit lay weltering in blood, their brains dashed out and dabbled with their long grey hair. Infants scarcely a span long, with their faces cloven with hatchets and their bodies ghastly with wounds."*

After he published the editorial his life was threatened, and he was forced to flee Humboldt County a month later. The Wiyots had inhabited the island since the 900's A.D.[51]

That same day the same mob was reported to have killed fifty-eight more people at South Beach, about one mile south of Eureka even though many of the women worked for the white families and many could speak 'good English'. Two days later, forty more Wiyots were killed on the South Fork of the Eel River and thirty-five more at Eagle Prairie a few days later. Those attacks nearly wiped out the tribe. Though the attacks were also widely condemned in newspapers outside Humboldt County, no one was ever prosecuted for the murders.

---

[51] In June 2004, the island was repatriated back into Wiyot hands.

While this event didn't take place in Trinidad, it shows the prevailing attitude about Indians throughout the general area at the time. The Tsurai people integrated themselves more than most other coast Indians and so had less trouble – many Europeans even took Tsurai women as wives.

**The Siege of Trinidad**

The Civil War dominated the national news in 1863, but in August of that year, the residents of Trinidad were preparing for "The Siege of Trinidad'. Colonel Francis Lippitt, who was then the commander of Fort Humboldt, received information that a band of Indians had taken possession of a timbered point of land about twelve miles north of Trinidad and had attacked some travelers, inflicting casualties.

It seemed clear that the Indians were attempting to cut off communication with settlements to the north. Company B set off on a forced march from the fort and arrived at Trinidad to find the residents there awaiting an attack at any moment. They had barricaded themselves in buildings and had a cannon set up on Golinda Street, expecting the worst. They had also rounded up all the local Indians and were holding them on the Head, and arriving ships were being held at bay... no passengers were allowed to come ashore.

The soldiers marched on north to the Indians' location, but found no one there. The command split their forces chasing the Indians through the hills, but lost the trail and never caught up with them. The only casualty was when one of the soldiers mistook one of his own men, Private Kershaw, as an Indian and shot him. Finally, they came upon a group of civilians who had found an Indian trail by accident while chasing a couple of white criminals of their own. The soldiers set off on that trail and eventually got their fight, killing about thirty Indians. The 'Siege of Trinidad' was officially over.

**The Battle of Christmas Prairie**

In 1863, word was received that a number of Indians were harassing local settlers midway between Bald Mountain Peak and Redwood Creek, northeast of Trinidad. Thirty-five troopers were dispatched from Fort Humboldt, arriving on Christmas morning, but found that about two hundred Indians were well entrenched in sturdily built Plank Houses. After a couple hours of serious fighting, it became clear that the Indians were too well-prepared and so the army backed off and the battle ceased while reinforcements were summoned.

More soldiers arrived later that day and brought a howitzer cannon with them that was put to immediate use. Boom! Bang! Direct hits! But the soldiers soon ran out of ammunition. Well, darn it! More ammo was ordered and troops were stationed to keep the Indians from escaping, but as they kept watch, the usual daily fog moved in. When the mighty army finally stormed the buildings, they found two dead Indians. All the others had escaped through the army lines in the fog. A hundred and twenty-five soldiers were sent to hunt the escapees down, but they were long gone. This became known as the Battle of Christmas Prairie and was one of the last big battles of the war.

Hostilities ceased in 1864, but the California Volunteers remained garrisoned in the area until the end of the Civil War in 1865. In general, across the country, Indians had been thriving for ten thousand years. It took the white man about sixty years in the 1800's to change everything for them.

## The Bald Hills

As I said, the war was fought in the Bald Hills, to the east of Trinidad. Why are the 'Bald Hills' called the Bald Hills? The Bald Hills are the ridges, between the Klamath River on the north to the Eel River on the south, and run from the eastern edge of the redwoods way up towards the main Coast Range. They're not really bald, but there isn't the dense forest land that covers the rest of the area so completely, either. Along the small streams on either side are plenty of small trees and shrubs. In certain seasons, the hills are lush with grasses and are a favorite place for deer and elk.

Actually, the widest part of the redwood forest is about just a bit north and east of Trinidad where the redwoods stretch about ten miles wide.

## Bull o' the Woods

Speaking of redwood trees... by 1860 Humboldt was the second ranking California county in lumber production, sawing thirty million board feet per year. At that time, the redwood forest covered more than two million acres of the California coast.

The main lumber being sawed up was redwood, spruce, and fir, and small quantities of cedar with most of the lumber being shipped to the San Francisco market. However, getting logs to the mills was a problem... they were huge!

In 1854, W. H. Steymast & Co., of Humboldt Bay, sawed a 'spruce-pine log' twenty-six feet long, which produced four thousand board feet of clear boards without knot or wind-shakes. Estimations at the time were that "There are trees of other woods much larger—for instance the redwood—that are estimated will turn out upwards of one hundred thousand cubic feet. A tree that big will build two houses, each two stories high and fifty feet square, furnishing all the square timber, planks, shingles needed. Four redwood logs, containing by actual measurement 26,902 feet of lumber, were hauled by a ten-ox team on a logging claim, a distance of three-quarters of a mile. It is claimed that this is the largest load ever hauled in the county by ten oxen. To give an idea of the size of the trees, we give an account of a tree cut down by a citizen of Arcata in 1855, which stood within two hundred yards of the Times newspaper office. From it a man built a house 24x30 feet, two stories high. The frame, siding, doors, windows and roof were made from lumber split from one tree. Also lumber to build a garden fence and out-house. He sold lumber enough to build his brother-in-law a one-story house."

At first, logs were moved using a 'jack screw', and were floated or towed in nearby rivers and bays. A jack screw was set beside the log, the screw was turned to jack the log up, and then a second guy would place his jack screw and continue to help move the log along. The two men working alternately could fairly quickly move the log any place that they wanted it to go.

Horses and oxen pulled logs longer distances on skid roads, and in some cases pulled wagons with a log or logs all the way to the mill. Logging railroads, which were primitive at first, finally began hauling logs to the mills. Some of the first railroads in the state were here in Humboldt County. I'll get to that in a bit.

The first redwoods were cut by two men with axes, sometimes taking as long as a week to take down a single tree. These guys must have had biceps the size of a normal man's thigh, although you can't tell it in the pictures.

Redwood tree stumps often 'swell' at the base, so the loggers would chop holes up where the tree wasn't quite so thick and stick a 'springboard' in the hole to stand on so they could chop and saw away at the tree. Standing on the springboard and swinging an axe had to have been an adventure. The board must have been jumping up and down with every swing and the faller was trying to balance himself as he raised the axe for another mighty whack at the tree. Yeah, that hardly looks dangerous at all. I'll bet more than one accidental 'swan dive' was taken from those boards.

Presumably, it was worth the ride so that they could get up to a point where the tree was a couple of feet less in diameter, though. We're talking trees that are twenty to thirty feet in diameter… and an axe makes a chop of about five to six inches at a time. You can see why there was no point in spending the time and effort sawing away just to gain a couple more feet of log. After all, there were redwoods all over the place… the forest was just lousy with them.

Standing on a Springboard

*"To be around when a big tree comes down is like being in an earthquake. There is a crack and whoosh sound, and then a tremendous thump that shakes the ground under you, and then an after-shock followed by absolute quiet, and the absolute quiet is deafening."* – That's how one crusty old logger described it.

As you might expect, this was dangerous work. Unfortunately, for the woodsmen, there were no arrangements for time off for injury or death. Men who were too injured to continue working, or if a man was even killed on the job, they were unceremoniously pulled off to the side out of the way and another man was hired on the spot from the group that was always present looking for work, and the job went on.

A logger who worked for Kallstrom's Logging Company in the Luffenholtz Creek drainage had a serious accident when removing a choker from a pair of logs and they rolled, crushing his legs. The logger was a tough old bird, though, and after he was replaced and left near the landing, he crawled uphill to the railroad and waited for the train which arrived later in the afternoon. While he waited, he applied a tourniquet, which was his belt, to his more seriously injured leg. Finally, hours later, the train arrived in Arcata where doctors made the decision to amputate the one leg, but he died before morning anyway.

As improvements were made in equipment, a good lumberjack could fell a smaller three-foot diameter tree in an hour. A five feet diameter tree took three and a half hours. Larger trees took longer. Ordinarily two men worked together, one on each side of the tree, using a 'misery whip'. The misery whip was a two-man saw, ten to twenty feet long.

Why didn't they just use a chain saw? Well, the 'osteotome' was invented by a German, Bernard Heine, around 1830 and had small cutting teeth with angled edges linked by a long chain that was moved by turning a wheel. But Heine was an orthopedist, having nothing to do with the lumber industry. His saw was for bones.

Another early chainsaw-type tool was an entire saw that moved back and forth when cranked and another called the 'American riding machine' that resembled a rowing machine with cutters on it. One claim states that a California inventor named Muir was the first person to put a chain on a blade to use for logging purposes, technically inventing the first logging chainsaw. However, Muir's invention weighed hundreds of pounds and required a crane to move it around... which wasn't very practical out in the woods. A steam powered portable saw was tried locally as early as 1875. The first experiment with a gas powered saw wasn't made until the 1920's in Eureka. That saw, a two hundred pound drag saw, was driven by a two cylinder, water cooled, marine type motor set at ninety degrees from its normal position. The machine sawed through a ten-foot log in four and a half minutes... and the crowd went wild!

Later, other Eureka brothers developed a lighter ninety-five pound drag saw.

In 1926, a German engineer, Andreas Stihl, invented the 'cutoff chainsaw for electric power' - the first electric chainsaw, and this was publicly accepted as the first real mobile chainsaw.

So; after the tree was down, it was cut – or 'bucked' - by a single man into saw-logs with a cross cut saw. After a while, they figured out that one man could make a longer cutting stroke than two men if they cut off the second handle. Once the logs were in a manageable length for transportation, horses and oxen were used to skid them from the woods to the waterways or loaded on wagons to get them to the mills.

'Skidding' just means to drag the logs out to where the loggers could load them. Skid roads were sometimes covered with small logs to make skidding easier. Mud was good, too.

Wages for working in the woods went something like this:
- Swampers (cutting skid roads and making landings and such) made sixty to one hundred dollars a month.
- Choppers made sixty-five to seventy-five.
- Sawyers and Chain Tenders made sixty-five to one hundred dollars.
- And Teamsters made a hundred twenty-five to a hundred fifty dollars per month.

In 1863 William Carson and John Dolbeer formed the Dolbeer and Carson Lumber Company. John Dolbeer became the inventor the steam donkey engine that replaced horses and oxen in the woods for skidding and changed the industry overnight. He first tried out his invention in 1881, and the device was patented in 1882.[52]

Horses and oxen have been forever grateful.

Carson went on to become rich and build the Carson Mansion in Eureka, but this is a story about Trinidad.

Oh, before I forget, the Bull o' the Woods was the foreman of a logging crew… and he was usually one tough son-of-a-gun.

---

[52] You can see a steam donkey at Fort Humboldt State Park in Eureka.

## Officially a Town... a City... no wait, a Town...

The claim is often made that Trinidad is the second oldest incorporated town in California. That's almost true...but not quite. So was it 1850 or 1870?

In 1957, Walter C. Stutler, Deputy Secretary of State, State of California, wrote in a letter that "Prior to 1883, when the Municipal Corporation Bill of 1883 was passed, most incorporations were effected by legislative acts. There was a period of time when incorporations were by order of boards of supervisors under authority of Chapter 113, Statutes of 1856. It was necessary that the population exceed 200 and that the petition to the board be signed by qualified electors and showing the metes and bounds of the proposed town. This act did not require any filing with the Secretary of State. Therefore, prior to 1883, our office relied upon the Statutes for dates of incorporation. Trinidad was never incorporated by legislative act. It is not, as far as we can ascertain, the second oldest municipal incorporation. It is possible the town operated under some form of local government not provided by law. Several towns were incorporated by legislative act in 1850 and these would have been older... officially."

Sure enough, if you look it up, the official years for incorporation for the towns in Humboldt are:[53] 1856 Eureka; 1858 Arcata; 1870 Trinidad; 1893 Ferndale; 1906 Fortuna; 1910 Blue Lake; 1965 Rio Dell.

So, while *founded* as a town in 1850, before the others, Trinidad was indeed *incorporated* by the Board of Supervisors of Humboldt County on November 7, 1870. These records are in the Humboldt County Courthouse.

Sacramento has the claim to be the oldest incorporated city in California, incorporated on February 27, 1850. In any case,

---

[53] From the Atlas of California, 1979; Pacific Book Center. Ned Simmons copy.

we remain today as one of the smallest incorporated cities in the state.[54]

Or as we like to say, "Trinidad is so small that on a map, it says Shown Actual Size."

What's the difference between a city and a town, anyway? A city is an incorporated municipality, usually governed by a mayor and a board of aldermen or councilmen. A town is an unincorporated community with no governmental powers. A village is even smaller than a town and a hamlet is on the menu at Denny's.

## Trinidad Becomes a City with a Lighthouse

In 1871, work finally began on the proposed lighthouse on Trinidad Head. First, workers built a road up the eastern side of the Head, and then began work on the lighthouse itself. The light was placed just twenty feet off the ground. Saaay what? Well, given the loftiness of its perch, on a one hundred and seventy-five foot cliff, they figured that a squat brick tower would do just fine. The tower and the keeper's dwelling, which was built about fifty yards from the tower, were finished over the course of the summer and fall, and on December 1, 1871, Keeper Jeremiah Kiler turned on the revolving fourth-order Fresnel lens for the first time.

The Fresnel lens is the 1822 invention of a French guy, Augustine Fresnel. Lighthouse lanterns had an oil lantern that burned constantly from dusk until dawn with no flashing or blinking like we think of them today. Tests showed that while an open flame lost nearly ninety-seven percent of its light, and a flame with reflectors behind it still lost eighty-three percent of its light, the Fresnel lens was able to *capture* eighty-three percent of its light. Because of its amazing efficiency, a Fresnel lens could easily throw its light twenty or more miles to the horizon.

---

[54] Or another way to put it is that as of 2014, Trinidad was the 14,719th largest city in the United States. We're movin' on up!

The 'order' – such as in 'fourth order' – just refers to the distance of the flame to the lens. 'Revolving' means that it revolved... but you probably figured that out on your own.

It was noted that the Trinidad coal-burning light had to be kept trimmed and burning for fifteen hours a day and that kept the keeper pretty busy. When the light was not in use, a curtain had to be drawn around the lens because the glass that was used would discolor in the sunlight.

Keeper Kiler faithfully stood watch over the light for seventeen years.

In 1898, Kiler's successor, Fred L. Harrington, who stayed on the job until 1916, oversaw the installation of a fog bell[55] on a rocky outcropping about fifty feet below the light. A clockwork mechanism was housed in a frame bell house just east of the bell, and weights were hung down the face of the cliff to power the whole contraption. The four thousand pound bell was struck at regular intervals by a heavy hammer, run by the clockwork mechanism. It was ingenious... except that the keeper had to wind the machinery every two hours! A second keeper was finally hired to help with the winding and trimming the light wicks.

The fog bell worked just fine for a couple of years, until the weight cable snapped, sending the weights plummeting down the face of the cliff. Look out below! To fix that problem, a wooden weight tower was constructed on a concrete foundation next to the bell house.

The grand sum of two hundred and fifty dollars was appropriated in 1899 for a telephone line to connect the lighthouse to Trinidad, and the Sunset Telephone Company was contracted to put in the redwood poles and string the wire. After about a year of use, the Lighthouse Board discontinued the telephone service, as the Sunset Company charged an annual rental fee of sixty dollars for the use of its equipment and the phone had "proved to be of no use to the Light-House Establishment".

---

[55] The original bell is the one at the Memorial Lighthouse.

It was interesting that they used a 'telephone' since telephones weren't anywhere near Trinidad at the time. The Sunset Telephone Company was a Seattle, Washington company willing to come all the way down here just to string a single, short line for the lighthouse. Apparently they felt with the loss of the lighthouse business, Trinidad as a whole would just have to wait for telephone service.

Trinidad itself had gotten wired in with a telegraph finally about 1877 or maybe even a bit earlier, but not telephones.

Harrington remained at the station for twenty-eight years before retiring in 1916 and being replaced by Edward Wilborg. The Coast Guard took over the lighthouse in 1939.[56]

## Do You Smell Smoke?

The same year that work started on the lighthouse, the Trinidad fire of 1871 burned down Rose Ann Sangster's hotel, the 'Occidental'. The fire started in a faulty chimney and spread quickly throughout the entire building.

Fires were fought by the town folk using the standard bucket brigade; getting water from watering troughs or wherever they could and passing bucket-full by bucket-full from hand to hand to get it to the fire. Water sources were the big problem, though, with no water lines or plumbing developed yet in those days and that's why fires got so big and did so much damage. Often, the best you could do was get out of the way, hope for the best and watch everything burn up.

The Sangster's had built the Occidental on Golinda Street, facing the bluff in the middle of town in about 1864. It was a grand three story pre-fabricated job brought by ship around the Horn[57] and assembled on the spot where it stood until the fire.

---

[56] The current lighthouse is up the trail/road on the east side of the Head. It was automated in 1974 and Coast Guard personnel lived there until 2000.
[57] Cape Horn is where the Atlantic and Pacific Oceans meet at the tip of South America.

Prefabricated houses were not at all uncommon back then.[58] For the early settlers on the north coast, it was an easy way to get established quickly when starting your own towns... 'easy' being a relative term.

I'm not sure what it cost to ship a house or hotel seventeen thousand miles around the Horn, but passenger service was six hundred dollars and took six months from the east coast to the west coast. One report says that it took approximately two years to order and have shipped a prefabricated house from the east coast. That means that it took some advance planning - as well as money - to come here and build a hotel. A full Masonic Temple in Benicia reportedly cost eighteen thousand dollars be shipped around the horn in the 1850's.

In any case, the townspeople were devastated to lose the hotel and rallied to gather and donate fifteen hundred dollars – a substantial amount in those times - to Rose Ann, a widow at that time, to rebuild, which she did. At least there was lumber available now unlike when the Sangster's first arrived so they didn't have to order another hotel from back east.

This isn't about the fire, but Rose Ann also married Warren Watkins, who worked on the lighthouse, in August of that year and from then on the hotel was called Mrs. Watkin's Hotel until 1881 when she sold out to Mike Hanrahan, who had another hotel in town. He ran it until it burned again in 1902, along with three other buildings. Hanrahan rebuilt the building, but this time it became a brothel with girls from Eureka until it burned again in 1913-1914... "Just as well," I can hear some of you saying.

That fire also took out the old Brick Store, Bob Phillip's saloon, and Sangster's Tobacco Shop.

---

[58] Prefab houses go back to the 1600's in America, but they really gained popularity in the early 1900's with the invention of 'kit houses'.

The Occidental Hotel on the Left – the Old Brick Store on the Right

Rose Ann Sangster arrived in Trinidad from Michigan in 1863 with her husband, Jabez, and her six year old son, Alexander. In fact, they arrived in the middle of the Siege of Trinidad. How's that for an entrance? It had been a long boat journey and Rose Ann was quoted at the time as saying, "I'd rather face the Indians than spend another moment on this damn boat!" She gave birth to another son, James, in 1865. Jabez died in San Francisco that same year... we don't know what he died of or why he died in San Francisco, but they had originally moved here on his doctor's orders because of 'ill health'. When her hotel burned in 1871, she married Warren Watkins and they went on to have children of their own; Martha, Mary and Warren Jr.

But this was supposed to be about fires... Squirrel!

Mike Hanrahan had started his own hotel, the Hanrahan Hotel, about the same time as the original Sangster's Hotel in the mid-1860's. It was also a prefab job and was also brought around Cape Horn on sailing ships, but it was more ornate and pretentious than Sangster's.

## Railroads and Roads and Cars... Oh My!

By 1858, freighting with large, specially built wagons had mostly replaced pack mule trains. The trips became a bit easier with farms and ranches along the routes providing lodging and meals for the freighters. Wagon trails improved, but still were atrocious, steep and rough, with difficult grades and hair-pin turns. As mining declined, freighting became more and more tied to the expanding lumber industry, supplying lumber camps and hauling logs until the short line railroads took over.

Early rail lines in Humboldt County consisted of logging 'railroads'. The logging railroad was made up of light rails tacked to flimsy ties and laid on a thin rail bed or over perilous wooden trestles sixty feet in the air. The lines often had curves of thirty degrees and grades of six, or eight or ten per cent, up which the small steam engines struggled valiantly. Logging steam engines were much smaller compared to what we think of when we usually think 'steam engine' and 'Iron Horses'. These were more like 'Iron Shetland Ponies'. Once logs were loaded, with a line of cars as much as eighty feet long, they were dropped down the grades with only hand brakes to rely on. The line could carry several trains operating on a single track and often without the aid of a dispatching system, too. No problem!

Most local operations used a 'Shay'[59] locomotive which had direct gearing to each and every wheel. The smooth, even flow of power enables the engines to negotiate twisting mountain grades.

One of the largest of the redwood trees known, the Lindsey Creek Redwood that grew out near Fieldbrook, was estimated to weigh between six and seven million pounds[60] and contained

---

[59] Invented by Ephraim Shay in the 1870's.
[60] That's about the weight of a Saturn 5 rocket.

over eighty thousand cubic feet of redwood when it fell over during a storm in 1905. This equates to about seventy-five hundred board feet of lumber. One of today's highway logging trucks carries about forty-five hundred board feet per truck. That means that a line of rail cars eighty feet long, fully loaded with green logs weighed approximately... you divide the tangent of the cosine and ...a lot... it weighed a lot... it was *very* heavy!

Line of Train Cars Headed to the Mill

The Trinidad Mill Company started out with a rail line with gravity fed cars. That means that the line had no engines – cars were dragged up to the logging site by mules, then after the cars were loaded with tons of redwood logs, they were brought back down using gravity to bring the cars to the mill in Trinidad. Have you ever fallen down and been reminded of the saying, "Gravity – it's the law!" The same applies to gravity fed rail cars. At times they would get away and go screaming down the hill. The Hooper brothers finally bought a steam engine, the *Sequoia*, and in 1880 had it shipped to Eureka on the Schooner *Alice,* and then brought up to Trinidad.

Getting it to Trinidad was the hardest part. They couldn't have unloaded it in Trinidad because of the lack of a pier for loading and unloading something anywhere near that heavy even though it was in pieces. The pieces were brought up in wagons and put together at the mill. They later renamed the engine *Trinidad,* and it remained in service with various other companies after the mill company closed until about 1934 before it was scrapped.

You can see how small the engine is... and engines like this one had to pull cars up grades and down hills. They were some kind of workhorse, that's for sure!

On December 15, 1854 the Union Wharf and Plank Walk Company built a mile and a half long pier to a deep water channel in Humboldt Bay near Union to load lumber schooners. Actually, Bryon Deming who had the mill with March, moved to Union and built the pier.... which ironically, helped kill off trade in Trinidad where his mill was. A wooden-tracked rail line serviced the pier using a horse as the locomotive at first. This line was the oldest working railroad in California. In 1875, the railroad was renamed the Union Plank Walk and Railroad Company, and a small steam locomotive, named the *Black Diamond*, towed lumber out onto the pier from the 1872 Dolly Varden mill owned by Isaac Minor.

Now, I've tried to keep most of this story in a timeline, even if the topic bounces around a bit, but some stories just need to be told all at once. So it is with the following:

In January of 1860, there was a rutted, but passable wagon trail between Arcata and Trinidad. All that was needed was a bridge across Little River, so one was requested. Discussion ensued.
April 1875: The wagon trail is wretched and just about impassable in places now.
June 1876: The stage line of Crogan and Cave made their first run on the wretched wagon trail.
August 1877: Contractor Nathan Daugherty signed a contract to build the bridge across Little River for $920.00.
December 1877: The wooden bridge is complete. We no longer have to go across the beach and risk high water and rough weather!
August 1878: Stages will leave Arcata at ten a.m. on Mondays, Wednesdays and Fridays, and leave Trinidad at eight a.m. on Tuesdays, Thursdays and Saturdays. Fares from Trinidad to Eureka are two dollars and fifty cents.
November 1878: The wagon trail is an 'elephant to deal with'! It is rough, circuitous, full of steep grades and exceedingly expensive to keep in repair… and wretched.
November 1880: Approval to build a new road is given and it is declared a public highway.
April 1881: The bridge at Luffenholtz Creek has been washed out. A proposed new bridge for a proposed new road below the current one is absurd due to the steep grade it will

take to get down to the bridge and back up to the old road. The bridge was replaced where it was.

November 1881: How about fixing the bridge across Little River that was washed out two years ago?

May 1882: Little River Bridge repair approved.

May 1883: No road built yet between Little River and Trinidad. Approved in 1878, declared a highway in 1880, surveyed; but only the bridge over Luffenholtz Creek was built... and owing to the stupidity of somebody... it was built several hundred feet off the survey in a place inaccessible to wagons so that a stationary engine will have to be placed to haul teams over the approaches.

May 1883: It is reported that the Road Overseer is out looking for the roads. It is doubtful if he can find them.

May 1883: There's a plea for a bridge over the Mad River. A loaded pack train with seventy-four mules had to be unpacked on the south side of the river so the cargo could be taken across on a flat boat, then the mules were swum across, then the whole shootin' match had to be repacked on the mules. This took a full day.

October 1883: Parties from Trinidad say the 'roads' have never been in better condition as recent rains have settled the dust admirably.[61]

February 1884: Approval was given for a bridge over the Mad River.

May 1884: The Trinidad wagon trail was partially repaired. Flaherty's Stage Line is ready to start passenger service.

September 1884: Work has begun on the Trinidad Road!

October 1884: Success! The Trinidad Road[62] and Mad River Bridge have been completed.

Whew! That only took twenty-four years... for cryin' out loud!

---

[61] There may have been just a bit of sarcasm in that statement. It's hard to tell...

[62] The old County Road follows Westhaven Drive and Stagecoach Road.

One of the Better Wagon Trails Past Princess Rock

Fires raged around Trinidad in 1867 damaging several railroad lines. All it took was time and money to replace them. It wasn't unusual for short lines to have wooden rails back then, when they used horses and mules to pull the cars. Those wooden lined burned very nicely. Fortunately, wood wasn't all that hard to find for replacement parts.

The fires had a lot to do with logging slash not being cleaned up at the time. 'Slash' is what they call branches and small trees left on the ground after logging. Once the railroads had metal rails, though, many fires were started by sparks from the wheels on those metal rails.

In 1875, John Vance built a sawmill near the Mad River community of Essex with a railroad to transport lumber from the sawmill to the Mad River Slough on Humboldt Bay for loading onto ships.

That was just a year before Custer had his dust-up with the Indians out in Montana. It didn't go so good for Custer. Vance had more luck with his railroad.

Vance's Humboldt and Mad River Railroad had three locomotives and connected with paddle-wheel steamboats from Eureka at the Mad River Slough. The railroad was incorporated as the Eureka and Klamath River Railroad in 1896. Andrew Hammond, for whom the popular local hiking trail is named, bought the railroad and sawmill on August 30, 1900.

On June 15, 1878, the Union Plank Walk and Railroad Company was reorganized as the Arcata Transportation Company. Union had changed its name to Arcata in 1860. The company's old side-wheel steamer, the *Gussie McAlpine,* was replaced by a sternwheeler named the *Alta* and the company kept adding track to local mills. In 1881 the Arcata and Mad River Railroad assumed control of the old line. They spent the next two years extending the rails further upstream on the Mad River until they reached the town of North Fork, renamed Korbel in 1891, and the Humboldt Lumber Mill owned by the Korbel brothers. Because of the initials of the line, it was cleverly nicknamed the *Annie and Mary.* Annie and Mary were either clerks working at each end of the line, or Annie and Mary Vintera, nieces of one of the Korbel Brothers. The story goes both ways.

A side note: the mill at Korbel was the first mill to use a kiln to dry lumber. It was all air dried before that... and air drying in our humidity and with our annual rainfall wasn't all that easy.

In 1883, the Korbel family bought the line which had about twenty-seven miles of track split between carrying passengers and logging track. The Korbels organized the company on December 29, 1891 as the Arcata and Mad River Railroad

Company. In the late 1880s, the A&MR line also carried lumber for the Minor Mill and Lumber Company of Glendale, which was near Blue Lake. In 1896 the line carried twenty-four thousand seven hundred and fifty-two passengers from town to town, and six thousand, four hundred and seventy-five tons of freight from four saw mills and two shingle mills.

The first known Humboldt County railroad accident with injuries occurred on September 13, 1896 when seven people were killed and twenty-three injured by a train falling through the Mad River truss bridge. Crashes out in the woods operations were a common sight, though.

Passenger train travel in Humboldt County in the 1890s was, shall we say, 'difficult'. The train stopped at every settlement along the way making a rail journey between Fortuna and Eureka an hour and a half event. The Eureka & Eel River Railroad ran from Eureka all the way south to Alton. That's a whopping distance of about thirty-five miles or so. If you needed to go further, you could transfer to the Pacific Lumber Company's train which would deliver you to Scotia, another five or six miles south. Anything past that required a horse. The trains were mostly for transporting lumber from the mills to the ports for shipping and supplies from the ports to the mills and logging camps.

The thirty-six mile Oregon and Eureka Railroad that was formed by Hammond's 1903 agreement with Southern Pacific was equipped with seven locomotives, two forty-eight foot passenger coaches, and a hundred and sixty-six freight cars. The railroad had two hundred and twelve freight cars by 1905, and was extended in 1906 to carry lumber from the Little River Redwood Company sawmill at Crannell. The Oregon and Eureka line was included in a Northwestern Pacific Railroad merger in January of 1907, and extended to Trinidad in June.

That was a long story just to mention Trinidad.

Northwestern Pacific passenger trains began operating to Trinidad in July of 1911. The train station was located near the rock quarry at Potato Rock. Trains came in and turned around on a turn table before being loaded with crude whale oil, boulders from the quarry – I'll get to those - shingles and shakes from the mills and livestock from the ranches. Mr. Wood was the first railroad depot agent in Trinidad. He was replaced by Walter Unsinger, and Bryan Hamilton was the last agent.

The Hammond Lumber Company was formed in 1912 and used some of the Oregon and Eureka rolling stock on logging branches off the former Oregon and Eureka main line. Hammond merged with the Little River Redwood Company in February of 1931. Northwestern Pacific ended service to Trinidad in March of 1935. Charles Kidder and his father claimed to be the last paying customers on the Trinidad line.

Northwestern Pacific completed a line down to Willits in 1914, and held a "Golden Spike" ceremony to celebrate. Unfortunately, they could only carry a limited amount of lumber on the single unstable line so it wasn't very profitable.

So; transportation in and out of Humboldt County remained a problem. Wagon trails and even county roads were nearly impassable in the wet winters as they turned to a bog of mud. This is an area that gets about forty inches of rain a year around Humboldt Bay and closer to fifty inches in and around Trinidad. Moving supplies in and out of the county was still only possible on any scale by sea.

Taking a stage around the county wasn't much fun, either. It was a three hour trip from Trinidad to Arcata in 1890. And you certainly had to plan ahead for a trip from Trinidad to Crescent City as it took eleven hours just to get there!

In 1903, Burr McConnaha owned and operated the stage and mail line from Trinidad to Requa City at the mouth of the Klamath River. He later purchased Flaherty's livery and stable in town. His brother, Clarence, took over the general store from Philetus Bell.

While the automobile industry began in the United States in the 1890's, it was Henry Ford's 1908 Model T that was the country's first affordable car. As already stated, highways were in short supply in Humboldt County at that time. However, the story goes that Harvey M. Harper drove the first auto through the redwoods in the winter of 1912; literally creating his own road around the giant trees so his Model T could make its way over the deeply rutted, muddy wagon trail that was all that existed at the time. He made the trip because it would have been outrageously expensive to have a car shipped to him for his new Ford dealership in Eureka. Now, there's a guy with foresight and incredible confidence in his own salesmanship abilities. But, as it turns out, even with the lack of passable roads in the area, Harper sold a number of cars to local residents in his first year in business. You go, Harvey! Harper Motors continues on today, a successful auto dealership just north of Eureka.

However, Harvey did not have the first automobile in the county. Back in 1899, J. G. Lovern, a wealthy shingle manufacturer in Eureka, ordered a horseless carriage from Illinois. It was shipped to San Francisco and brought to Eureka on the steamer *Pomona*. It took a full month and cost Mr. Lovern a total of two thousand five hundred and seventy dollars, including freight costs. Apparently shingle mills could be very profitable.

The McConnaha brothers already had the stage line in Trinidad, but with the introduction of autos, they added Pierce Arrow stages and used trucks in good weather and horses and wagons in bad weather. They sold the stage line in 1924 to the Pickwick Company... who later sold it to the Greyhound Stage Company. Burr McConnaha then started up the Humboldt Motor Stage Line, which he sold to the Humboldt Transit Company in 1955! The Humboldt Transit Company is alive and well today.

McConnaha's Stage Line

## Where'd the Town Go?

In 1881, the Hooper's sold out their Trinidad Mill Company to the California Redwood Company, who closed everything up by November of 1886. The logging rail lines were abandoned. What wasn't closed up was destroyed by fire, so that only a couple of small shingle mills remained in the area. A lot of men were out of work, and another era was ended in Trinidad.

With the loss of jobs came the inevitable loss of population. The town began to look a bit ragged.

Alexander (Sandy) Sangster built a two story hotel that he called the Ocean View up on the plateau above town on Trinity Street in the early 1890's.[63] Slowly, businesses started moving up the hill to relocate with him. About 1900, Frank Mc Daniel built the Trinidad Hotel that lasted until the 1950's.

---

[63] His hotel was on the site where the Eatery now stands.

Sandy Sangster also built a store in 1904, up on the plateau by his hotel. Unfortunately, he had to file for bankruptcy in 1905 and he died of pneumonia in 1906.

His younger brother, Jim and his brother-in-law built a hotel at Big Lagoon around 1890. Unfortunately for Jim, in 1893 when a friend's horse team got stuck making a crossing at Big Lagoon, Jim went to help but was knocked unconscious in the process and drowned. He had just been married ten days earlier to Edna Wellcock.

James and Alexander's mother, Rose Ann, died in 1919.

By the early 1900's, the old town of Trinidad was just about unrecognizable. Occasional fires took out so many buildings that only Ingraham's Hotel, Bell and Hansen's old shingle mill, a general merchandise store, two of Child's stores and the Occidental Hotel remained down on the slopes. 1904-1905 saw a push of the last few holdouts so that by 1906, almost all of the original buildings were gone.

That didn't mean that the city of Trinidad was finished, though; oh, no, not by a long shot. It just moved up the hill a bit. Edwards Street[64] became the new business district with stores facing the bay and lined up close enough so that if one burned, they could all burn… which, of course, they eventually did…

Buildings that hadn't burned earlier were carefully taken apart so that the lumber could be reused. I believe that was more for economic reasons than environmental ones, though. In any case, re-use of lumber was a common practice.

I'm guessing that the blacksmiths of that time did a dandy business in making nails back then, too. Trinidad certainly wasn't alone is burning down more than once. Check out any old town and they'll have a colorful history of fires. Wooden buildings and no water supply will do that.

---

[64] Running along above the bay.

Edwards Street – McConnaha's Store

## Doc, My Arm Hurts in Three Places. Well, Don't Go In Them Places!

The number of doctors in the county continued to improve... unlike today as we lose more doctors every day... but that's another book... still in all, it wasn't healthy to be sick back then. In 1890, common causes of death included: accidents – probably the number one cause of death, and surprisingly, drownings were not uncommon at all - consumption (also called tuberculosis), cancer, disease of the heart, pneumonia, softening of the brain,[65] dropsy, diphtheria,

---

[65] That one's got me worried.

Bright's Disease, and old age – which was in a person's eighties.[66]

## Watch the Cow

Lest you think it was all bad news back then here's a clip from the 1899 Daily Humboldt Times:

"Captain James C. Franson has the watch on exhibition belonging to William Owens of Trinidad, which was swallowed by a bovine about seven years ago and but recently recovered by the owner. The timepiece does not look any worse for its experience, soundingly it being in good condition yet." Oh, thank goodness!

Enough of that... back to bad news...

## The Big Storm

March 12, 1904. "The heaviest and fiercest windstorm of the season occurred here Wednesday evening when a violent southeast gale was blowing accompanied by rain. At Trinidad the high trestle leading to the wharf was razed to the ground." The Trinidad Mill Company was long gone by then, though.

## Do You Smell Smoke?

Wednesday, September 12, 1908. It was a warm, fog free day with a bit of a breeze blowing off the ocean. The breeze fanned embers from a fire previously thought 'out' in a log jam at Kallstrom's mill in Luffenholtz. By mid-afternoon, a good sized blaze was going with a forty mile per hour wind, and it was headed right for the town of Luffenholtz on the bluff above. Since none of the towns had any firefighting equipment

---

[66] Taken from Humboldt County death records at the County Clerk's office.

due to inadequate water supplies, the only plan was to evacuate in circumstances like this, so that's what the residents did... in a hurry!

Families headed towards Trinidad or down to the beach to walk across to Little River. Some men tried to reach the town from the north, but the bridge over Luffenholtz Creek was already afire. All anyone could do was wait for the flames to die out on their own and then go see what was left.

Nothing *was* left... except charred stumps and piles and piles of rubble. Not a single structure escaped; houses, the store, the post office, the train depot and cookhouse, and the mill were gone...Charlie Kallstrom's shingle mill, which was just built in 1905, and even the mill on Houda Point were gone...and with them, all jobs were gone. The orchards of fruit trees and huge vegetable gardens were gone... everything. The fire burned clear down to Dow's Prairie, across Little River. The town never recovered.

Poor Charlie Kallstrom; his mill was a model of innovation, as noted in a 1908 copy of Woodworker Journal for Machine Wood-workers. He had invented and installed a band shingle mill that was a revelation in shingle sawing. His mill was a large affair that looked like a regular lumber mill, only turned horizontally. The wheels were eight feet in diameter with two bands, teeth down, running on each side. It was quite the contraption... and it all burned up in the fire.

The mill and loading facilities at Houda Point also burned. Brothers B. A. and J.P. Houda built their mill in 1895 and Charlie Kallstrom ran it for them, but it burned in 1899. Partners Hansen and Larsen built a replacement, using equipment from the Jolly Giant Shingle Mill in Arcata, and that replacement mill is the one that burned in the 1908 fire. The Houda boys loaded shingles aboard ships using a crane on the rock that sticks out into the cove where ships anchored below to take on the loads. In 1902, the *Rodondo* steamer took on seven million shingles in a single load from there. But the facilities all burned up in the big fire.

The San Francisco Call reported on September 25, 1908:

*"Towns and valuable timber lands are being wiped out completely and as yet there is no indication that the miles of flames will be checked. The Little River mill has lost its $10,000 electric light plant which had just been installed. Two deaths have been reported so far with the loss of hundreds of head of cattle. Dozens of families have not been heard from although they are believed to have reached safety. Refugees are coming out of the clearings from the burned timber land by the score carrying only a few personal effects. Charlie Kallstrom's mill at Luffenhotlz has suffered a devastating loss of thousands of cords of bolts and much dry timber. The mill at Fieldbrook also burned and there is another fire at Stone Lagoon with many smaller fires burning around Trinidad."*

As devastating as that fire was, it wouldn't be the last:

- The Trinidad post office burned in 1910.
- Fires in 1913 took out five railroad trestles near Trinidad.
- The wharf burned in 1914, and as already noted, the school burned in 1914, too.

A couple of houses burned up in 1926… and fire struck again in 1928 when the entire block between Trinity and Edwards Street burned from a fire that started in Pinkham's Saloon. The fire took out the telephone switchboard that was in Saunders' store as it burned so no one could call out for help. It took residents four or five hours to put out the fire.

Speaking of Saunders' store, Glenn Saunders, future owner of the store, was four years old at the time of this fire. Glenn passed away in 2015.

Consider that all these wooden structures back then had burning oil lamps and wood stoves for heat and cooking. It's a wonder there weren't even more fires!

# The Last Ship

It was noted that the last tall sailing ship, the *Alutules*, dropped anchor in Trinidad Bay in 1910. The sailors were a good natured bunch who came up to the Good Templars Hall and put on displays of native dances for the folks in town.

President Howard Taft was not notified of the event.

# More Mills

Thirty-five year old Edward Schnaubelt emigrated to the U.S. from Austria in 1890. He briefly panned for gold before settling in Trinidad, buying a tract of timber from the Lagoon Timber Company in Big Lagoon and opening a shingle mill, the Humboldt Shingle Company in 1900. Edward hand tooled his own saws, bands and belts, and organized his neighbors into a co-op and went to work. Unfortunately, business dried up in the depression of 1908 and his mill was forced to close. When the bank in Eureka foreclosed on the property, Edward fought the proceedings for several years and finally lost in court. This didn't set well with him and he refused to leave the property becoming somewhat of a nuisance to his neighbors.

In May of 1913, a newly formed shingle mill — not sure which one - purchased the mill's machinery from the Lagoon Lumber Company and started the process of moving it out. Edward was mightily displeased by the entire proceedings and re-entered the closed mill one night to reclaim some of the tools and equipment and was shot to death by a night watchman hired to 'protect the property'... or to shoot Schnaubelt, whichever comes first.

There are two stories about the night watchman, named Kelly; one story says that he was acquitted of anything, claiming that Schnaubelt had appeared over him with a lead pipe in his hands and he shot in self-defense. The other story says that he got two years in the state penitentiary for manslaughter. In either case, Edward is buried in the Trinidad cemetery and his headstone reads – 'Murdered by Capitalism'.[67]

In 1910, the McConnaha brothers built their shingle mill on the east side of Trinidad just a couple of hundred yards south of the quarry and ran a four mile aerial line out into the woods, up towards Strawberry Rock. Think about that… a four mile aerial line that brought shingle bolts flying through the air like a ski lift. They say it looked like a giant spider's web made of cables in the forest with the aerial lines and the shingle bolts dangling from them as well as support lines holding everything up.

There's an accident waiting to happen. You know some of those lines had to break once in a while and you'd better not be anywhere around when cables went snapping through the air like an out of control whip!

And who had the job of stringing the bolts to the line to keep it all moving at a steady pace?

Bucking and cutting the bolts was hard work… especially handling the 'Blue Sinkers' which were cut from the butt cut of a tree. That meant that they were big and heavy! All the bolts, whether for shingles or railroad ties had to be sledded to a landing so that they could be strung on the aerial line for transport to the mill. The sleds were pulled by horses or mules.

McConnahas' Bolt Camp was up near Strawberry Rock and consisted of a cookhouse and several cabins which were on skids to make them easier to move around in the woods. Most woods operations had camps like this, but in this case, because of the depression, many men chose to walk to work to save the cost of room and board at the camp. And the walk home could be several miles…. after a day of wrestling bolts…

The mill and logging operations were quite the going concern until the 1929 depression. The mill couldn't survive that… especially after yet another fire – this one set by a disgruntled employee – pretty much burned the whole mill to

---

[67] His grave is at the top of the graveyard next to the wooden fence.

the ground. Combine that with the depression and there was no point – or money – to rebuild.

The shingle mills were a constant fire hazard with all the sawdust and metal machinery parts grinding together; not to mention disgruntled employees. It's a wonder any of them survived for very long.

Cutting Shingle Bolts, Ready to Send to the Mill

Speaking of the depression, between 1920 and 1939, sixteen of twenty remaining mills around Humboldt Bay closed.

Charlie Kallstrom, whose mill at Luffenholtz burned in 1908, leased some property from Carson and Dolbeer and opened a new shingle mill above Fieldbrook around this time, around 1910, also. This mill had two Hanson shingle machines, one shake machine, and a tie machine. Charlie's mill was still operating as of 1912.

As I mentioned earlier, a lot of the shingle mills were small and didn't last long. It's hard to get information on some of them. The Mayvilla Shingle Mill employed seventy to eighty men somewhere 'just north of Trinidad' sometime in the early 1900's. That's all we have on that one. Don't know who owned it or how long it lasted.

## The Lighthouse and the Wave

You may have seen dramatic pictures of lighthouses being engulfed by crashing waves, so it may not seem unusual that a twenty-five foot tall lighthouse might get hit by a wave... unless that lighthouse is perched on a one hundred and seventy-five foot high cliff.

The one building in Trinidad that was never destroyed by fire seems to be the lighthouse. The most notorious event connected to it, though, was a huge storm wave that struck the Headland in 1914.

Keeper Harrington recorded the following account of the incident in the station log:

*"The storm commenced on December 28, 1914, blowing a gale that night. The gale continued for a whole week and was accompanied by a very heavy sea from the southwest. On the 30th and 31st, the sea increased and at 3 p.m. on the 31st seemed to have reached its height, when it washed a number of times over (93-foot-high) Pilot Rock, a half mile south of the Head. At 4:40 p.m., I was in the tower and had just set the lens in operation and turned to wipe the lantern room windows when I observed a sea of unusual height, then about 200 yards distant, approaching. I watched it as it came in. When it struck the bluff, the jar was very heavy, and the sea shot up to the face of the bluff and over it, until the solid sea seemed to me to be on a level with where I stood in the lantern. Then it commenced to recede and the spray went 25 feet or more higher. The sea itself fell over onto the top of the bluff and struck the tower on about a level with the balcony, making a*

*terrible jar. The whole point between the tower and the bluff was buried in water. The lens immediately stopped revolving and the tower was shivering from the impact for several seconds....*

*Whether the lens was thrown off level by the jar on the bluff, or the sea striking the tower, I could not say. Either one would have been enough. However, I had it leveled and running in half an hour. About an hour later another sea threw spray up on the level of the bluff, and the constant jars of the heavy sea was much over normal during the night and the whole of the next day. On the 3rd, the sea moderated to some extent, but a strong southeast wind and high sea continued until the 5th. During the 26 years that I have been stationed here, there has at no time been a sea of any such size as that of the 31st experienced here: but once during that time have I known the spray to come onto the bluff in front of the tower, and but twice have I seen sea or spray go over Pilot Rock."*

The lighthouse was one hundred and seventy-five feet above the water and the lighthouse is another twenty-five feet high and the light was extinguished by a wave that splashed up over the whole thing!!

Apparently it was a rogue wave that hit the Head at that particular spot. Harrington's statement of 'a sea of unusual height approaching' points to a rogue wave, also. Rogue waves are defined as being twice the height of other waves at any given time. So with other waves breaking over Pilot Rock, a rogue wave could reach the lighthouse.

The combination of a rogue wave and the prevailing ocean currents explains why there was no other damage along the coast. You would have thought that a wave that big would have taken out the Tsurai village too, but no other coastal damage was reported from that storm.

And think about the fact that Keeper Harrington was *in the lighthouse* when the wave struck. Can you say 'heart attack!' But no, he calmly straightened everything up and re-lit the lamp before going home to tell his wife about the excitement. Just another day at work.

No, not me. No, sir. Thank you, very much!

A Wave Splashed Up and Hit the Lighthouse!

Those bluffs are covered with brush now, but standing next to, or in the tower, you can still get a good feeling for how high the lighthouse is above the ocean. The original lighthouse still is in operation and is open a few days each year for tours.

## Keep on Movin' On

The Humboldt County Federated Women's Club decided on a worthy project in 1913 and placed the current concrete cross on Trinidad Head, marking the location of the original wooden cross placed by the Spanish in 1775.

Granite Cross on Trinidad Head

I already mentioned the lighthouse wave in 1914 and that the wharf caught fire and burned up. That was a bummer. Too bad they didn't happen together so that the wave could have put out the fire.

Oh, and World War I broke out that year, too. Albert T. Tighe, Mose Saunders and Glenn W. Chaffey went off to war. Actually, Mose wasn't a Trinidad boy when he went to war, but he became best friends with Glenn Chaffey during their stint in the army together. Mose lost a leg in the fighting, but Glenn lost his life on the last day of fighting in the Verdun forest. When Mose got back and healed up, he came up to Trinidad from his home in Stockton to pay his respects to the Chaffey family. When he arrived, he met Glenn's sister, Mae, and that was it. He married her and stayed, making the Saunders family a mainstay of Trinidad life for years to come.

The town, in 1914, looked like this: entering Trinidad up the steep grade from Stagecoach Road onto the intersection of Main and Trinity Streets, there was the blacksmith shop. Directly across Trinity Street was where the schoolhouse was located. Heading South on Trinity where the Town Hall currently stands was a twelve foot long watering trough where horse drawn rigs with steel-banded wheels, which were good on the gravel roads, could water their horses. Where West Street intersects, there was a saloon and Child's Stable. Across the street from that was Sangster's Hotel. Edwards Street was the main business district with a wooden boardwalk, the post office, grocery store, and bar, all facing the bay. All in all, a pleasant place to visit.

The big watering trough was also for cows in town. Cows and calves had the right to graze the streets, but not bulls or steers. I don't explain them... I just report. It was each person's responsibility to keep the cows out of their yards and gardens. That's why so many houses had nice big picket fences.

In May 1915, the Mount Lassen volcano erupted. This was just a few months after the Trinidad lighthouse episode with the giant wave. There appears to be no connection between the Trinidad lighthouse and the volcano blowing itself to smithereens except for the timeline.

Also in 1915, the Trinidad Ladies Civic Club decided that the town could use a little culture, so they formed Trinidad's first library. The first location was in a small shed behind the Riecke home. The shed was spruced up and heated with a wood burning stove purchased for five dollars and the ladies raised money to cover the dirt floor with a wooden one. Mrs. Lottie Riecke Pinkham was the first librarian. There was no note of how many books they started with.

Telephones started up in Trinidad about 1915, too. Boy; did that speed up social media... or as they called it then – 'gossiping'... although, there was only one phone in town and that was in McConnaha's store.

Families often enjoyed a picnic at the picnic grounds up by the train depot through these years. An earlier picnic grounds was where the Ocean Grove Restaurant/Lodge/Bar on Patrick's Point Drive now stands. There was a boardwalk a full three feet wide that ran from the pavilion where dances were held, all the way to the train station. Crowds would often come by excursion train for special events. There were picnic tables and areas for throwing horseshoes and other games during May Day and the Fourth of July. Horse drawn carriages took people to and from town if they wished. Every community had its fiddler who could play every song 'by ear', and other musicians would join in. Other dances were held at the Good Knights Templar Hall or if someone built a new barn... or even cleaned out an old one... they had a 'barn dance'. Children accompanied parents to all events. There were no babysitters back then.

## The Last Yurok in Tsurai

In 1916, the last Yurok Ner-'er-ner' left the village of Tsurai. Most Yuroks who had lived there had either passed away or moved in and around Trinidad proper already. No one knows for sure who the very last villager was, but there's a story that says that Humpback Jim and his wife were the last.

Humpback Jim married a woman named Skarap, who was from Hewer,[68] where her first husband had been killed by a raiding party of Chilulas. Skarap was so devastated at losing her

---

[68] Hewer was at Stone Lagoon, north of Trinidad.

husband that she learned to pray people to death. She actually became feared by people who got on her bad side for her ability to pray people to death. Skarap went to the site where her husband was killed and gathered sand from the footprints of the raiding party and prayed over the sand repeatedly until all twelve of the raiders were dead... within a year!

Humpback Jim, wasn't bothered by her reputation, so he married her and brought her to Tsurai where they lived in their plank house.

One story says that Jim died in either 1913 or 1914, and Skarap was brought out in 1916. Within a short time, she died and was buried someplace other than in the Tsurai village graveyard. Another story says Jim likely wandered off and Skarap moved back to her home village.

In any case, the village was empty. The village that was... what? – several hundred years in the making - was no more. No fanfare... no ceremony... it was just over and life moved on.

## One Last Tsurai Story

I'm not sure of the date of this incident, but it must have happened in the late 1800's and it's about how Trinidad Pete single-handedly almost saved Tsurai and the whole world from being destroyed. And no, I didn't make this up.

Pete actually lived about a mile from Tsurai Village. One day, while he was visiting some relatives in Tsurai during a storm, the villagers could hear and see a near-white sea lion on a rock out in the bay. The sea lion was up on the highest point of the rock, sleeping, and groaning with his head pointed upward towards Heaven, as his body swayed around in a circular motion. It was decided that, being a white sea lion, he was praying for the world to come to an end, so he needed to be killed immediately.

Pete, seeing no other volunteers, stepped up and said that he would do it. He swam two hundred yards out to the rock and tried to stab the sea lion, but his hands were freezing,[69] and the sea lion's hide was tough, so his knife slipped off and cut four fingers of Pete's hand, severing the tendons. The sea lion woke up and immediately dived off the rock. Pete had no choice but to swim back to shore; but the world wasn't destroyed.

Trinidad Pete died in 1934 and is buried in the Trinidad Cemetery.

## Westhaven is Born

March 30, 1916 – The Humboldt Standard Newspaper:

*"Plans for a summer resort at Luffenholtz Beach to be known as West Haven and to include not only summer homes but a big tourist hotel, golf links, tennis courts and other amusement features have been launched by the Coast Land and Investment Company in charge of William E. Wisby. According to Mr. Wisby the plan of the company is to sell lots in the tract, first offering them to Humboldt County people and later to the outside communities."*

Obviously this grand plan never quite happened, but the name Westhaven did stick to the general area where the town of Luffenholtz was.

## Trinidad Keeps Going

In 1917, the Trinidad Town Hall[70] was constructed. The original building is still being used on a regular basis.[71]

---

[69] Water temps run about fifty-three degrees even in summer.
[70] Located directly across from Trinidad School. It's on Trinity Street.
[71] Trinidad's Born in a Trunk Melodrama Company performs there from time to time. They weren't around by quite a number of years when the building was constructed, but I wanted to mention them in here someplace. They got started in the 1970's.

Fires destroyed five and a half trestles plus the bridge over Luffenholtz Creek on the County Road in 1917, too.

On the heels of World War I, which ended in 1917,[72] a proposal was made for a west coast military highway, which may have been the precursor to the building of Highway 101 – the Redwood Highway – several years later. Somebody was thinking ahead.

1918 saw Mose and Mae Saunders take over the old General Merchandise store from Clarence McConnaha. That store just hung in there and hung in there.

Clarence McConnaha and John Spinas built a modern garage and service station that was serviced by the local Standard Oil Company distributor in 1924. It was located at the corner of Highway 101 and Main Street. They provided full service in those days, checking oil and washing windshields. Gas was about twenty-one cents a gallon.

Pinkham's Saloon was the place to hang out during the roaring twenties in Trinidad… well, until it burned down. It's said that at one time, back in the old days, Trinidad's streets were paved with gambling cards.

## Thar She Blows!

The whaling industry brought new income to Trinidad when the Hammond Lumber Company and Little River Redwood Company decided to build a whaling station here. They actually began work on the station in 1912 with foundation and rock blasting preparation, but the proceedings were interrupted by World War I. Those wars will do that. The station sat unfinished until 1920 when, after spending two hundred and fifty to three hundred thousand dollars, it was finally completed. The California Sea Products Company under

---

[72] Me own sainted mother, Thelma, was born that year. B'gosh and Begorrah… and we're not even Irish.

Captain Fedrick Dedrick took a twelve year lease to run the operation.

From 1920 to 1926, whales were caught locally and processed at the whaling station in Trinidad.[73] Whales were caught by steam-powered whaling vessels — the SS *Hawk,* SS *Hercules,* and SS *Port Saunders.* These vessels hunted the seas along the north coast making one to three trips per day to catch local whales. It was a process called 'shore whaling' because they didn't go to sea for months hunting Moby Dick.

*"At the first streak of dawn the whalers man their boat, six to a boat, and proceed to the whaling ground. Here they carefully scan the water for a spout. Suddenly one sees the wished-for column of mist, and cries out, 'there she blows!' Then all is activity and the boat is headed for the whale and the guns are made ready to fire. Having arrived within shooting distance, which is about forty yards, the harpoon, connected with a long line, is fired into whatever part of the animal is visible."*

They used steam-driven harpoons to kill their prey and then quickly filled the whales with air to keep them afloat for the trip back to Trinidad where they were hauled up a ramp using Dolbeer's steam donkey to winch them up into the whaling station where they were flensed – a process where they were stripped of blubber and skin - and then the carcass was processed by the thirty-five local, mostly Scandinavian, workers. Sometimes there would be two or three whales floating and tied to the pier waiting to be brought into the plant.

Only one fatality occurred at the station while it was open. Twenty-two year old Hobart Haynes was working with a cutting machine that malfunctioned and the blades flew off, decapitating him. No occupation was safe from accidents.

---

[73] Located where the pier and Seascape restaurant are now.

Trinidad Whaling Station

A nearly eight hundred foot pier was run out to Prisoner Rock where the water was fifty feet deep[74] to facilitate unloading and processing the whales. That pier didn't last past the whaling station's existence.

Whale oil, of course, was the chief product and even though oil lamps weren't used as much across the country, whale oil was still used by companies such as Procter & Gamble to manufacture their finest soaps. The Standard Oil Company also used whale oil combined with mineral oil for making lubricants. Even oleo margarine, invented in 1813 by a French chemist, was made from the lowest grades of the oil. Yum! The meat was turned into chicken feed if it was fresh enough. A double floor under the cutting room floor caught all the excrement and blood which was boiled down along with the intestines and made into fertilizer. The bones were run thru pressure cookers where the last drops of oil were extracted and the bones, after being dried, were sent to the sugar refineries to be used in refining sugar (I don't *even* want to know...).

---

[74] Or as we all know now, that's just over eight fathoms.

The whale oil was transported in rail tank cars from Trinidad to the company's other station in Field's Landing,[75] which is just south of Eureka. As many as one hundred tank cars per season were transported.

The Trinidad lighthouse keepers often served as a lookout for the faint white puffs of whales blowing as they came up for air, indicating the presence of gray whales migrating along the coast. As many as twenty-nine whales a week were hauled ashore in the bay for processing, which produced a somewhat offensive odor. They say you could smell Trinidad before you could see it, in some cases from as far away as Orick - twenty miles away. Most Trinidad residents were hugely relieved when the whaling operations ended in 1926.

It was reported that in the last year of operation, the station recorded catches of twenty-one Humpback, seventy Finback, twenty-five Sei,[76] one Sperm, and one Gray Whale (in 1924, there was one Blue Whale catch).

The plant closed in 1926 due to 'unsanitary conditions'. How could they tell?

About the whales;

Humpback whales are a species of baleen whale… which means that they filter out food such as krill, from the water by lunge-feeding or gulp-feeding. Adults range in length from thirty-nine to fifty-two feet and can weigh seventy-nine thousand pounds. The humpback has a distinctive body shape, with long pectoral fins and a knobby head. They're known for their spectacular breaching behaviors, which makes them popular with whale watchers. Found around the world, humpback whales typically migrate up to sixteen thousand miles each year. Their diet consists mostly of krill and small fish.

Finback whales, that today we call Fin whales, are the second longest whale in the world - Blue whales are bigger - measuring up to ninety feet long and weighing thirty to eighty tons in adulthood. Fin whales are non-migratory, or at least

---

[75] That plant operated until the 1950's when it burned to the ground!
[76] Pronounced *'say'* as in "Say, that's a big whale!"

nobody knows their migration patterns, and they can be found all over the world, except at the poles, although they prefer offshore areas.

Gray whales are smaller than Finbacks, measuring forty-nine feet long and weighing fifteen to thirty-five tons, and they prefer coastal areas where they feed along the sea floor. Gray whales are typically found on the west coast of North America and migrate with the seasons, spending their summers in the arctic and winters around Baja California. They live fifty-five to seventy years. They begin their southern migration sometime in October, leaving the Bering Sea for the warmer waters of Baja California. It takes them two to three months to make the journey, and they can be spotted off our coast in November. The northern migration begins in February and lasts through April. The whales, including mothers and calves, travel closer to the coast on the northbound journey, so this is usually the best time for whale watching from shore.

Sei Whales are also a baleen whale. They inhabit most oceans and adjoining seas, and prefer deep offshore waters. They migrate annually from cool and subpolar waters in summer to winter in temperate and subtropical waters. They stretch sixty-four feet long and weigh as much as twenty-eight tons.

Sperm whales are the largest of the toothed whales and are the largest toothed predator. Mature males average fifty-two feet in length but some may reach sixty-seven feet, with the head representing up to one-third of the animal's length. Plunging to over seven thousand feet, they are the second deepest diving mammal – the deepest diving is the Cuvier's beaked whale. The head of the sperm whale contains a liquid wax called spermaceti, from which the whale gets its name. Spermaceti was used in lubricants, oil lamps, and candles.

## Killed By an Apple

After the whaling plant was closed, they still had a watchman to keep an eye on the equipment. Sig Hansen, veteran watchman, was on duty one afternoon when he noticed a truck parked under a walkway in the plant. He walked over the walkway, approximately thirty to forty feet off the ground, and saw that the truck was loaded with apples. Calling down to the driver, he requested that an apple be tossed up to him, which the driver was happy to do… except that the toss was short and the apple landed on the edge of the walkway. Sig reached out to grab the apple before it rolled away, lost his balance, and fell from the walkway hitting the ground with a mighty thud. He died shortly after hitting the ground from a broken neck and other internal injuries.

The actual structure was torn down in 1930, leaving just the office building and old smokestack. The boilers were sold to the Western Condensing Company for a milk processing plant down in Petaluma. The smokestack was torn down in 1949 to make room for a parking lot and the office was condemned and removed in 1961.

## Asphalt Comes to Trinidad

The roads in and out of Humboldt County were a system of wagon trails, with four main outlets in and out: Two roads to the south to inner and coastal Mendocino County, a road east to Trinity County, and one headed north through Crescent City then on to Grant's Pass. These roads were extremely unreliable, however, as they were often at the mercy of Humboldt County weather.

The Humboldt part of the Redwood Highway actually got started in 1915 or so, when local legislative bodies slowly approved contracts for grading large stretches of the highway. That helped, but by the 1920's, the roads were still dirt and mud and there were twelve wooden bridges between Trinidad and

Big Lagoon... and you had to drive all the way around Big Lagoon to get on north... and then take a ferry across the Klamath River...

By 1925, the highway was being paved; coming north, it ran along Clam Beach on what is now Little River Road, continued along what is now Scenic Drive, and ran through Trinidad heading on north along what is now Patrick's Point Drive. That's like saying that "The highway ran past where the old Johnson barn was until they tore it down, then it turned where that big dip in the road is." But, by golly, we had a highway! It was paved and everything.[77] Paving the highway was a huge step. It used to take four days to get from Eureka to San Francisco, but after paving, it only took fourteen hours. Zoom – zoom!

Of course, with the city traffic to our south, we'll be back up to a fourteen hour trip before long.

# Rock on!

Unlike Trinidad Bay, Humboldt Bay was always in need of jetties to protect the entrance to their bay. Jetties had been built as early as 1889, but they always washed out and needed to be re-done several times. And so it was when the North jetty needed repair again in 1924.

Trinidad to the rescue! Ta-ta-taaaa!

A rock quarry was established on the east side of Trinidad – curiously enough, it's located on Quarry Road - to provide rock for the jetty. In fact, Potato Rock seemed to be the perfect location since the train depot could be placed right nearby and rail cars could easily be loaded for the trip to Humboldt Bay.

Potato Rock was a well-recognized local feature that was originally named by the Yuroks with a name that loosely translated to "where-they-gather- potatoes."

---

[77] The current fancy freeway was put in during the 1960's.

The rock from the quarry is called 'greenstone'. It's an old deep-water ocean lava flow that has been pushed up to and through the surface. It's a very hard rock, making it a great material for the jetty because it can take the pounding surf without breaking up.

The quarry had several whistles that sounded to let folks know a blast was about to happen so everyone could take shelter from the rocks falling from the sky. We Trinidad folks are a polite bunch, always looking out for one another like that.

The first load of rock was shipped in July of 1924, but it was ten days late because a fire had taken out a trestle … and then upon arrival at the jetty, three loaded flat cars derailed. Not an auspicious start. But soon enough tons of rock were being transported daily from the quarry.

If you'd like to visit Potato Rock, you'll have to go out to the jetty. Where Potato Rock used to be is a hole in the ground that we just call 'The Quarry'.

Train Depot and Potato Rock

## Oh, the Power!

Electricity finally made it to Trinidad in 1937. We may be slow, but we're... sorry... what was I saying? Other Humboldt County towns got a bit of a jump on us with that one.

As of 1878, the residents of Humboldt County lit their streets and homes with gaslights. Small local companies like the Eureka Gas Company and Eureka Gas Works provided fuel. However, gas was not the only source for Eureka; in 1883, the Excelsior Lumber Mill on Gunther Island in Humboldt Bay generated electrical power for carbon arc lighting to provide nighttime illumination at its mill.

Eureka proper was the first to use this newfangled thing called electricity. Eureka's first power company, Humboldt Light and Power Company founded on October 23, 1885, was owned by the Vance Mill and Lumber Company. The power plant, attached to the mill, was located on Waterfront and G Streets in downtown Eureka. Naturally, the first business to have arc lights was the Vance Hotel, which had eight two-thousand candlepower arc lights installed. However, in 1892 a fire completely destroyed the Vance Mill and Humboldt Light and Power Company plant. As a result, Humboldt Light and Power sold their electric distribution system and customers to Eureka Electric Light Company.

On March 21, 1894 Eureka Electric Light Company was consolidated into a new company, Eureka Lighting Company, which became Eureka's sole provider of gas and electricity. Their plant was located on the southwest corner of First and C Streets, adjacent to the Occidental Mill. The steam electric power plant was powered by four boilers that burned sawdust and mill waste. However, without a way to catch hot embers emanating from its four smoke stacks, three small fires damaged the plant and a fourth completely destroyed it.

Jumping ahead since this particular story isn't about Trinidad; after World War II, electricity was supplemented by the steam electric plant of the *SS Donbass III*, a World War II

Russian Lend-Lease tanker that had broken in half in the Bering Sea. The stern of the tanker was tugged down to Eureka, beached, cleaned up, and wired into the Eureka electric system. The General Electric Company turbine-generator was in excellent shape, and in January 1947, the SS Donbass III Power House went on line.

They also had a nuclear power plant in Eureka that operated from August 1963 to July 1976 when concerns about previously undiscovered seismic faults, combined with more stringent regulations required after the Three Mile Island accident, rendered the plant unprofitable. It was shut down for refueling and seismic upgrades in July of 1976, which dragged on due to changing governmental requirements. PG&E cried 'Uncle' and announced plans to permanently close the plant in 1983. In 2004 they announced that three nuclear fuel rods were unaccounted for due to conflicting records of their location. *What?* The fuel rods were never actually located, although PG&E investigators believe that they got everything when they finally removed the entire kit 'n caboodle in 2012. There, I know I feel safer… them darned big city people.

Trinidad residents, being of sound mind, waited until they had perfected this gimmicky electricity stuff and brought in electric lines in 1937. "I heard that that stuff can be dangerous! You know that plug thing there on the wall… DO NOT lick your fingers and stick them in there to see what happens, I can tell you that for sure!"[78]

Electricity made it to the Trinidad lighthouse in 1942. As a result, in 1947 the fog bell was replaced by compressed air horns, and the lens was removed in favor of a modern beacon. Two years later, a replica of the tower, the Trinidad Memorial Lighthouse[79], was built in town on the bluff overlooking the

---

[78] Personal experience.

[79] 2018 Update – Due to soil erosion on the bluff, the Memorial Lighthouse has been moved down to the foot of Edwards Street to the parking lot for the beach and the pier.

bay, and the original lens was placed in the lantern room. That's the original bell next to it, too.

The Trinidad Head Lighthouse is still active, with a fancy new LED light. The old drum-type Fresnel lens is in the Trinidad Museum. A pair of fog signals are stacked next to the fog bell house, which is the only remaining bell house in California.

## Standard Oil

Yep, Trinidad had its own Standard Oil company plant in the 1920's and 30's. It wasn't exactly a big refinery; it was the local distributor's plant located about two miles southeast of town with a couple of big tanks. Located conveniently right on the rail line, rail cars could deliver gas and then pick up loads of cattle and sheep from the corrals right next door after loading other cars with gravel from the quarry to the north and whale oil from the processing plant. Cattle drives and sheep drives down the old county road were a common sight around here, all headed to the corrals from ranches at Orick and the open pastures around the Bald Hills. Head 'em up and move 'em out! Everybody sing…"Rawhide!"

And that reminds me about the story of:

## The Legend of Judas and the Sheep

Judas was a goat. That's not a philosophical statement of any kind… Judas really was a goat. The story goes that one of the local sheepherders owned Judas and used him to lead sheep drives down to the corrals by the Standard Oil yard to be loaded on the train. It was a fairly common sight to the folks of Trinidad in the late 1920's and early 1930's to see Judas calmly leading a flock of sheep down the trail from their pastures, along Old County Road and all the way right up the chute into a waiting boxcar, and then he would leap out the open door on other side where there was no ramp while the sheep stood there wondering how they were supposed to jump out like that. "Hey, Judas," the sheep would call to the goat who had led them there... then the boxcar door would slam shut behind them as they stood flat footed and wide eyed; and Judas would walk away to collect his bag of oats, never looking back.

## Passing of an Era

It's certainly worth a mention that Eliza Lindgren passed away in 1940. Her grandfather was Mau, the last rich man of Tsurai. Born in 1836, Eliza was the last medicine woman of Tsurai. The Ner-'er-ner' were known as strong healers and medicine people... and Eliza was the last official medicine woman. She built a dancehall in the town of Trinidad, where square dancing was a big hit with villagers and townspeople alike. Her philosophy was, "Now that we're all here, we've got to get along together," and she believed that dancing together was a big step towards getting along together... she was a healing woman. The local fiddler would strike up a tune and the caller would let loose with his patter call and Indians and whites would allemande and promenade around the hall together... just like Eliza hoped they would.

I never knew Eliza, but heck; I think I miss her, too.

Eliza's grandson, Axel, made the canoe that's on display in the Trinidad Museum, as well as a couple of others in the 1980's to replace a number of canoes that were lost in the 1964 floods. I'm happy to say that I often stopped and visited with Axel as he worked on one of them in the field/pasture just past the current Trinidad Bay Trading Company on Main Street. He was quite the storyteller.

I'm also happy to say that there's still a field/pasture on Main Street in Trinidad.

## Do You Smell Smoke?

Fire broke out in 1936 just north of Trinidad. This one, they called "The Big One." The flames burned down to the shoreline and were so intense that they even started fires on brushy rocks offshore. Several thousand acres of timberland were destroyed.

There was a big fire up on the Head in 1943, too. They just stood back and watched that one burn itself out. It spared the lighthouse but took out the popular dance floor that was just above the old cross location.

Another fire, this one over seven thousand acres, burned in 1945 from Crannell to Big Lagoon. It was noted that more than three hundred men were working the fire in the Abalone Beach area alone. This fire destroyed the mill at Crannell and took out the trestles to the mill at Big Lagoon.

And the rebuilt school burned again in 1949.

And that's when Trinidad decided that they might need a fire department... in 1949.

## The War Years

Early in the years of WWII, a major military base was built three miles north of McKinleyville. It had a seven thousand foot runway and could accommodate the largest bombers of the time. The base was considered ideal for research on fog dispersal methods such as powerful search lights, gasoline fires, and infrared lights to facilitate safe landings in the fog. Turns out that you can't disperse fog... you can only practice landing in it.[80]

A squadron of dive bombers used the sand spit at Big Lagoon as target practice; using sand bag mock-ups of bombs. Machine gun practice was held using offshore rocks as targets. The six hundred and forty acre former Trinidad bombing target

---
[80] Today it's our California Redwood Coast-Humboldt County Airport.

and air-to-air gunnery range was acquired by leasehold condemnation on January 10, 1944 and was terminated on March 4, 1946.

Three blimps stationed at McKinleyville were used for scouting enemy submarines. One sure sighting and sinking occurred off Turtle Rock, near Patrick's Point, with another 'maybe' off the entrance to the Mad River. A Japanese sub sank a merchant ship off Eureka. The disabled ship floated past Trinidad and beached at Crescent City.

The Johnson brothers, Greg and Jimmie, were the first to enlist from Trinidad. They rushed to the recruiting offices to join the air force. Greg interviewed first and was immediately accepted into pilot training. Jimmie interviewed next and when asked what training he had that might apply to the air force, he said, "I worked in the woods and I can chop wood."

When the recruiting officer said that the air force didn't have much use for a skill like that and maybe the army would be more appropriate, Jimmie pointed out that they had just accepted his brother. The recruiting officer said, "Yes, but he told us he had training as a pilot."

Jimmie nodded and said, "Yeah, but I have to chop the wood before he can pile it."

There is no actual corroboration for that story, either… or any evidence that there were any Johnson brothers…

A number of Trinidad boys did serve though, and we thank them:
Chuck Lindgren
Gordon Lee
Carl Rimby
Glenn Saunders
Elrid Spinas
William F. Woodcock
Williard T. Woodcock
Henry Boyes

Deepest apologies if I missed any names.

The only mainland bombing of the U.S. by the Japanese in WWII took place near Brookings, Oregon, about sixty-miles north of Trinidad in September of 1942. Incendiary bombs were dropped by a plane brought over on a submarine to start forest fires, but the area was too wet and no fires were started.

During the war, the telephone switchboard in Mose and Mae Saunders' store on the old Redwood Highway, which is Patrick's Point Drive now, was manned around the clock since the Coast Guard stationed on the Head were on twenty-four hour submarine watch. Mose was on the board during the day and Eldrid Spinas had the night shift until he was called into service. Then Glenn Saunders took over until he got called up, too. They had a cot next to the switchboard, so it wasn't too bad.

Bud Forbes was often stationed on the Head with Japanese airplane identification manuals, just in case.

## The Pier

In December 1944, Earl Hallmark bought all the property owned by the Hammond Lumber Company in Trinidad, including all the property between Ocean Avenue and the Head. Earl had a plan. He was able to purchase a bunch of pilings that had been part of the war effort, but never used. He then hired a local contractor, Tom Hull, to drive the piling into the rocks where the old whaling station had been. Only, the rocks kept breaking the steel points that the contractor was using. They pondered this a while, then just sharpened the pilings themselves and viola'! A five hundred and seventy-five foot pier was born.

Earl then built a saltwater tank, about eighteen feet by twenty-eight feet to hold live crabs for sale... but the tank's pumps kept clogging because of the silt and debris, so that idea was abandoned. Then in 1949, he built a one hundred and ten foot long cannery at the end of the pier. After one year of losing money, he gave up on the idea of a local fish processing plant, too.

In February of 1960, a light breeze out of the west turned into hurricane force winds in four hours. The wind was so hard that it blew foam from the north around Trinidad Head like a blizzard. In fact, the foam was so dense, that the Head couldn't even be seen.

On the same day, a huge ocean swell crashed on shore. It was the only time in the history of the pier that water washed over the top of it. The swell was so powerful that sea water rolled over the road at the foot of Edwards Street and down the parking lot into the bay on the east side of the peninsula.

The next morning, there were six crab boats remaining out of fourteen moored in the bay.

In 2012, the Trinidad Rancheria, who now owns the pier, completed a project to build a whole new structure. It looks very nice.

## Earthquakes!

Yes, we experience earthquakes in Trinidad. We're listed as a high earthquake risk, with a total of two hundred and seven earthquakes since 1931. Within the city, the Trinidad Fault (part of the Mad River Fault Zone) was designated under the Alquist-Priolo Act of 1972. The zone encompasses about sixty acres, or nineteen percent of the land within city limits.

Yeah, we have our faults… but we're good people!

The USGS database shows that there is a 77.6% chance of a major earthquake within fifty miles of Trinidad, CA within the next fifty years. The largest earthquake recorded within thirty miles of Trinidad was a 7.3 Magnitude in 1980, so we're about due.

But, you have a nice day!

## The End?

This is certainly not the end of Trinidad. The point just broke off of my pencil, so this is where I'm stopping the book. The population of Trinidad has continued to ebb and flow with the economic times, dropping as low as ninety-nine in 1945 and climbing clear back up to over three hundred now... now being 2016.

Fires continued to plague the town. In 1953 the Trinidad Hotel burned. That's the one that Frank McDaniel built in 1900. He sold it to Albert Ehreiser who changed the name to the 'Sea Breeze' during World War I, but changed the name back to the Trinidad Hotel after the war. In 1955 it burned again and was completely destroyed. Motels and travel trailer parks took their places as tourism became the town's economic driver. We've even had a couple of fires in the trailer parks.

In 2015 we had a strong El Nino that warmed the ocean waters and domoic acid formed so that the crab season had to be cancelled. It's always something.

At least we got some rain this last winter (2015-2016) after a big drought.

The old general merchandise store changed hands, locations, and names a few more times, but it remains, now in the form of Murphy's Market. Ironically enough, the Trinidad Rancheria now owns the boat basin, including the pier and restaurant. They have a big casino, built in 1986 down off of Scenic Drive, too.

Trinidad became known as a haven for artists and craftspeople. We have a big annual Fish Festival with a craft fair and fish feed in June every year. Trinidad also hosts the annual Trinidad to Clam Beach run. There's a nationally known eight and three quarter, five and three quarter, and three mile run that includes a stretch along the beach and a crossing of Little River... through the river... yes, your feet get wet.

And there's quite a few of us old retired people around. We try not to get too excited by much of anything while managing to keep the story of Trinidad alive.

Come visit us… or thanks for visiting… whichever applies.

## Trinidad Sawmills

1851  March and Deming build a mill for Loeffelholtz

1852  March leases Loeffelholtz mill

1853  March and Deming build their own mill on Mill Creek

1853  Mr. Krutschmitt leases Loeffelholtz mill

1854  Freshet destroys Loeffelholtz mill – not rebuilt

1869  Smith and Daugherty build mill at other Mill Creek – later named McConnaha's Creek

1875  Hooper Brothers buy out Deming and March as well as Smith and Daugherty and form Trinidad Mill Company

1881  California Redwood Company buys out Hooper brothers

1886  California Redwood Company forced to close all operations

1886  The old Deming and March portion of mill burns

1892  Bell and Hansen build mill by Trinidad Head

1895  Kallstrom builds mill for Houda brothers

1899  Houda mill burns – Hansen and Larsen rebuild it

1900  Edward Schnaubelt builds mill at Big Lagoon – closes 1908

1905  Kallstrom builds mill at Luffenholtz

1908  Fire destroys Kallstrom and Houda Brothers mills

1910  McConnahas build mill by quarry - closed about 1930 by depression and fire

Trinidad: Looking Back From My Front Porch

# Map

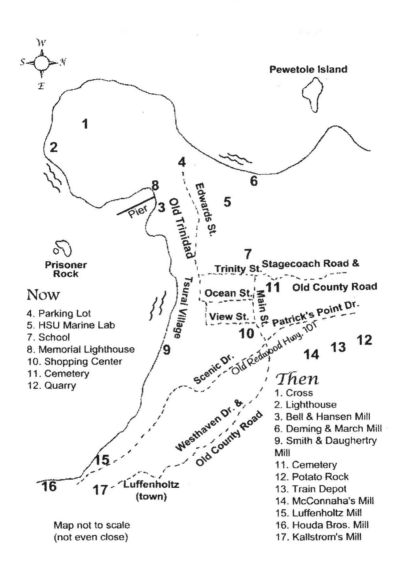

## Nautical Terms

Are you new to the ocean? Do you want to fit in during your visit with us? Then here are some nautical terms for the beginner. Most explanations are given in layman's terms, however, when you see this symbol:

there will follow a technical point for the really curious/geeky person in your group.

**What's a 'Tide'?**
Tides are the rise and fall of sea levels caused by the combined effects of the rotation of the Earth and the gravitational forces exerted by the Moon and the Sun. Generally, there are four tides a day: two high tides, and two low tides. It takes about six hours to go from a high tide to a low tide, then another six hours to go back up to high tide. The variation in height between the tides depends on location, season, and astronomical phenomena; sometimes the variation is only a few feet, while on other occasions it has been recorded to be as much as fifty feet!... but not around here.

This is because at the point right 'under' the Moon, the water is at its closest to the Moon; so it experiences stronger gravity and rises. On the opposite side of the Earth, the water is at its farthest from the moon; so it is pulled less. As the Earth moves more toward the Moon than the water does it causes that water to rise (relative to the Earth) as well. In between, the force on the water is diagonal or transverse to the sub-lunar, resulting in low tide. Told you it was technical!

**What's a 'Tidal Chart'?**
A tidal chart is a vital navigational aid, especially when maneuvering ships close to shore or into harbor. A

miscalculation in the tides could result in an accident such as running aground (that's a bad thing!). Fishermen who go out every day have tide charts relevant to their local area to assist them in deciding when to go out and where to travel.

Shore fishermen use them to know how high (or low) the water will be on the beach. You can pick up a tidal chart in most any local store.

## How deep is a 'Fathom'?

Officially, a fathom measures six feet (1.8 meters) in length. If fish are running at thirty fathoms, then they are one hundred and eighty feet deep.

The fathom is an ancient unit of measurement, dating back at least to the times of Ancient Greece. The use of the old English term *faethm* for 'outstretched arms' to discuss the measurement appears to be quite old, with the adoption of "fathom" for taking nautical soundings occurring in the 1600s. Typically, a knot would be made at each fathom length of rope, allowing sailors to count off the fathoms as they dropped the rope to the bottom.

## How far is a 'Nautical Mile'?

A nautical mile is equal to about 1.15 land miles, or 6080 feet.

## How fast is a 'Knot'?

Knots measure the speed of ocean vessels (or the wind at sea). A knot is one nautical mile per hour, so a ship traveling at five knots is traversing five nautical miles per hour.

5 knots = about 5.75 land miles per hour. So if you're whipping down the highway at 65 mph, you're going the equivalent of 74.75 knots. Slow down, I told you, you were going too fast!

To measure the speed and distance of a ship, knots were tied into a 'log line.' This line was thrown overboard, an hourglass was tipped, and the knots were counted. When the sand ran out, the counting stopped, and a general speed was determined.

**What's a 'Gale'?**
A gale is a very strong wind; however there are conflicting definitions of how strong. The U.S. Government's National Weather Service defines a gale as thirty-four to forty-seven knots (thirty-five to fifty-four miles/hour) of sustained surface winds.

Other sources use minimums as low as twenty-eight knots and maximums as high as ninety knots. Through 1986, the National Hurricane Center used the term gale to refer to winds of tropical storm force for coastal areas, between thirty-three knots and sixty-three knots. The ninety knot definition is very non-standard. A common alternative definition of the maximum is fifty-five knots

**What's the difference between a 'ship' and a 'boat'?**
Generally speaking, a ship is a larger craft capable of enduring long ocean voyages. A ship is also capable of carrying a boat. I'd go with whatever the skipper *wants* to call it.

**What's a 'Schooner'?**
A schooner is a sailing vessel with two or more masts. The most common type, with two masts, were popular in trades requiring speed and windward ability, such as slaving, privateering, blockade running, and offshore fishing

## What's a 'Brig'?

A brig is a sailing vessel with only two square-rigged masts. Brigs were seen as fast and maneuverable and were used as both naval warships and merchant vessels. And yes, the brig is also the jail on a ship... or boat... or whatever.

## What's the difference between 'Port' and 'Starboard'?

Port is the left side of the vessel as you face the bow (the front) and starboard is the right side as you face the bow. Just remember that "port" has four letters and so does "left".

Vessels at sea do not actually have any 'right of way'. They are in the position of being the 'stand on' vessel or 'give way' vessel. This means that at no time should any vessel actually navigate its way into a collision situation, and the rules are clear that no one in command of a vessel should assume a "right of way" and should at all costs avoid a collision. Consider two ships on courses that intersect. The rule is that the ship on the port side (the left) must give way.

## What's the difference between 'Bow' and 'Stern'?

The bow (like you take a bow after singing a song... not like a bow in your hair) is the front of the vessel. The stern is the back of the vessel.

## What's the difference between a 'Harbor' and a 'Port'?

A harbor is a sheltered body of water which can be used as a shelter for ships. Harbors fall into two basic types. Natural harbors are geological features created by the landscape. Artificial harbors are created through the use of piers, jetties, and other man-made features.

A port is a facility which allows ships to load and unload cargo. A port usually includes support for ships and boats including repair areas and stores for provisioning and stocking vessels.

TEST: If the port is on the port, where's the port? Trinidad people know that 'Port' means that the red wine is kept in the left side of the cabinet.

Technically, Trinidad Bay is a 'Roadstead', which is a sheltered offshore anchorage area for ships, not as protected as a harbor.

## What's the difference between a 'Wharf,' a 'Pier,' and a 'Dock'?

A wharf is a structure built on the shore of, or projecting into, a harbor so that vessels may be moored alongside to load or unload or to lie at rest on one side of it.

A pier is a structure built on posts extending from land out over water, used as a landing place for ships on either side of it. A pier can actually be used as a wharf.

A dock is the space or waterway directly adjacent to a pier or wharf, used for "parking" a ship while in port. It's open on three sides. If you're "Sittin' on the Dock of the Bay" as Otis Redding sang, you're sittin' in water.

## What's a 'Slip'?

Remember, this is about nautical terms so I'm not referring to the women's undergarment or to what happens when you step on a banana peel. A slip is the space between two piers and is open only on one end. A slipway is a sloping ramp used to bring vessels in and out of the water. A boat ramp is a slipway.

## What's a 'Mooring'?

A mooring is the act of securing a vessel by anchor or tying a vessel to a wharf or pier at the dock. A mooring line is the rope used to tie a boat to the wharf or pier or a buoy.

## What's a 'Buoy'?

A buoy is a device which is designed to float on the water, either in the open ocean or in a navigational channel such as a bay or river. In a heavily trafficked area, buoys may be used to mark out shipping lanes, ensuring that boats know where to go thereby reducing the risk of collisions. A buoy can also be used as a mooring device, allowing boats to anchor themselves without needing to be attached to a wharf or pier. Some divers and casual sailors take advantage of mooring buoys to anchor their boats while they dive, swim, or fish.

## What's the difference between 'Waves' and 'Swells'?

Let's start with waves. Waves are caused by the action of the wind across the surface of the sea like blowing on a cup of coffee. Sea waves are usually made up of a number of waves of different lengths kind of jumbled up on one another.

Swell is caused by storms or depressions out in the ocean. These weather effects cause swell like throwing a pebble in a pond would cause ripples. Swells are usually straight and long and they travel long distances across the water maintaining their power until they get broken up into smaller waves as they approach shore.

## What's a 'Rogue Wave'?

A rogue wave (also known as a 'sneaker' wave) is a large wave that appears 'out of the blue' and can be large enough to drag a person off the shore.

Rogue waves are relatively large and spontaneous ocean surface waves that are precisely defined as waves whose height is more than twice the other waves at any given time. Therefore rogue waves are not necessarily the biggest waves found at sea, but they are surprisingly large waves for a given sea state.

Rogue waves are a very real danger. Heed the saying to "never turn your back on the ocean." You cannot predict a rogue wave! And yes, we have them around here.

### What's 'Surf'?

Surf is waves breaking in shallow water or on the shore. It's what you go wading in at the beach — you go wading in the breaking waves.

If someone goes surf fishing, they are generally standing on the shore, fishing near the shore in shallow water where the waves are breaking.

Surf: riding a board on the waves, dude! It's like, a totally cool thing to do.

### What's a 'Breaker?

Breakers are waves that crest or break into foam. When you look out and see the white tops of waves near the shore as they build up and turn over, those are breakers.

### What's a 'Tsunami'?

Sometimes called a tidal wave, but that's very misleading. Tsunami waves go to the depth of the ocean unlike regular top waves. When the tsunami wave approaches land, the wave gets bigger as the sloping land creates shallower water forcing the wave upward.

You often hear of tsunamis caused by offshore earthquakes.

### What's a 'Jetty'?

A jetty is a device constructed out into the water rising to just above the surface to help control currents and provide protection for a channel at an inlet. While jetties usually can't stop a current, they may stop some beach erosion, helping areas along the beach keep their sand in the general area.

Jetties are often constructed of large boulders or manmade concrete shapes.

## What's a 'Spit'?

No... not the obvious. A spit is a sandy landform found off coasts. At one end, a spit connects to land, while at the far end they exist in open water.

A spit is a type of bar or beach that develops where a re-entrant occurs, such as at cove's Headlands, by the process of longshore drift. Longshore drift (also called littoral drift) occurs due to waves meeting the beach at an oblique angle, and backwashing perpendicular to the shore, moving sediment down the beach in a zigzag pattern.

## What's the difference between a 'Sand Bar' and a 'Shoal'?

A sand bar is a raised deposit of sand or other sediment caused by waves or currents.

A shoal is the same kind of deposit of sand or sediment but is big enough that it provides a hazard to the navigation of watercraft.

Bar crossings at bay inlets can be dangerous because the sand is always shifting in height and width.

## What's a 'Rip Current'?

A rip current occurs when there is a build- up of excess water between a sand bar and the beach. The water wants to flow downhill through the sandbar but it is blocked, building up pressure. The pressure is released through the point where the sand bar is weakest. This creates a hole in the sand bar where all of this excess water flows through at a very fast rate. Anything or anyone caught in the pull of the rip current will be pulled out past the sand bar until the pressure is alleviated.

If you are caught in a rip current, do not panic and do not try to swim immediately back to shore. Swim parallel to the shore. You should be out of the rip current within thirty to one hundred feet or so and then you can swim towards shore.

**What's an 'Undertow'?**

When a wave hits the beach, its force can often cause people to fall down. Once they have fallen, the wave will recede and pull them back into the water. Undertow is a very weak current that draws excess water back into the deeper ocean. It will not pull you under and keep you there. When you are pulled into the water, simply stand up and walk back to shore. Myths attributed to undertow come from the realities of rip currents.

**What's the difference between a 'Lagoon' and a 'Slough'?**

A lagoon is a body of comparatively shallow salt or brackish water separated from the deeper ocean by a shallow or exposed sandbank, or similar feature.

A slough (pronounced 'slew') is a secondary or narrow channel in a shallow salt-water marsh, usually flushed by the tide.

**What's a 'Head'?**

Ooooh, a tricky question… yes, a Head is the bathroom on a ship or boat, and it refers to your noggin, but I was referring to the piece of land. A Head, or Headland, consists of a point of land which thrusts out into the water, so that it is surrounded by water on three sides.

Typically, Headlands are characterized by being very high, with a sheer drop to the ocean or to a small beach.

## What's the difference between a 'Bay' and a 'Cove'?

A bay is an area of water mostly surrounded by land. Bays generally have calmer waters than the surrounding sea, due to the land blocking some waves and often reducing winds.

A cove is a circular or oval coastal inlet with a narrow entrance.

Generally speaking, a cove is a smaller bay. Again, I'd go with whatever the locals call a body of water.

## What's the difference between 'Leeward' and 'Windward'?

Windward is the direction upwind (toward where the wind is coming from) from the point of reference.

Leeward is the direction downwind (or downward) from the point of reference. If you are on an island, and the wind is blowing from the west, then the west side of the island is windward, which makes the east side of the island leeward.

## What's a 'Sea Stack'?

A sea stack is a pillar like mass of rock detached by wave action from a cliff-lined shore and surrounded by water. While on the beach, you may notice huge rocks that jut toward the sky. They stand out from the beach formations such as the headlands or they may shoot out of the water, looking completely out of place. The single column or columns of rock is called a 'sea stack'. The stack is a rock structure that is formed by a natural process – erosion.

# ABOUT THE AUTHOR

John is on his fourth career in life: he spent twelve years as a firefighter, then six years touring a two-person melodrama show with his wife Sheryl, then eighteen years supporting adults with developmental disabilities, and now as an author. He's still trying to decide what he wants to be when he grows up.

So much to do, so little time!

His materials on supporting adults with developmental disabilities are currently being used in forty-eight states and four other countries. And many of his close personal friends have read his fiction books.

You can check them all out at www.mosscanyon.com.

Made in the USA
Lexington, KY
16 September 2019